runes

runes

Martin Findell

The British
Museum

Martin Findell has asserted the right to be identified
as the author of this work.

First published in 2014 by
The British Museum Press
A division of The British Museum Company Ltd
38 Russell Square, London WC1B 3QQ
britishmuseum.org/publishing

ISBN 978-0-7141-8029-8

Designed by Bobby Birchall, Bobby and Co.
Printed and bound in China by C&C Offset Printing Ltd

The papers used by the British Museum Press are recyclable products
and the manufacturing processes are expected to conform to the
environmental regulations of the country of origin.

The majority of objects illustrated in this book are from the collection
of the British Museum. The British Museum registration numbers for
these objects can be found in the corresponding captions. You can find
out more about objects in all areas of the British Museum's collection
on the Museum's website at britishmuseum.org.

Frontispiece Detail from a runestone at Rök, Östergötland, Sweden.
9th century. H. 382 cm; W. 138 cm. The inscription contains a long
verse text, part of which is written in code (see p. 65). The meaning
is the subject of ongoing debate among scholars.

Contents

What are runes?

Runes are a form of alphabetic writing – that is, a writing system in which each symbol represents a sound. Unlike the Roman and Greek alphabets however, runes were (chiefly) only used for carving rather than for writing manuscripts and were therefore made up of a series of straight lines to aid carving.

Runic writing has been in use in various parts of northern Europe since at least the second century AD, and probably earlier. We do not know exactly when, where, why or by whom runes were first created. They are perhaps most popularly associated with Scandinavian culture of the Viking period (c.750–1050), but even before this, runes were known in Britain, the Low Countries (the coastal region of north-western Europe, consisting of Belgium, the Netherlands, and Luxembourg), parts of Germany and France, and a small number of inscriptions have been found in south-eastern Europe. The inhabitants of Anglo-Saxon England developed their own form of runic writing in the seventh century, but it had almost completely died out by the eleventh, well before the Norman invasion in 1066. In Scandinavia, on the other hand, the use of runes

continued into the late Middle Ages, and in some localities into the modern period.

Like any other kind of writing, runes served many different purposes over the long period of their use. People used them for labelling their property or their handiwork; demonstrating their social status or political authority; sending personal messages; and writing prayers and charms. The texts can be formal or informal, skilfully or casually carved, simple or complicated. We have inscriptions that express people's sense of loyalty, piety, affection, sexual desire, pride and playfulness. In both Scandinavia and England, runic characters were also used as the basis of riddles and secret codes; then again, we find some that are utterly incomprehensible. Some of these seem to be genuinely meaningless (linguistically, if not culturally): it seems that the visual appearance of writing, or an imitation of writing, was important in itself. Other apparently nonsensical inscriptions may have served a magical purpose; but the realm of rune-magic has been the focus of much ill-founded speculation, and we must treat it with caution.

The etymology of 'rune'

The word 'rune' has a long history. Many inscriptions, some of them quite early, contain the formulaic text 'NN wrote [the] runes'. It is not entirely clear whether the word (*rūnōz* in the language of the early Scandinavian inscriptions) means 'runic characters', or 'inscription, text', or both. It is sometimes singular and sometimes plural; the singular form (*rūno*) obviously does not refer to a single character, so here at least it must mean something like 'NN wrote this inscription'. Where the word occurs in inscriptions, it only ever seems to refer to writing, but many people have attached great importance to its supposed original meaning.

In Gothic (a now-extinct Germanic language, which we know about chiefly through the Bible translations made by the missionary Wulfila in the fourth century AD), the word *rūna* is used to translate Greek *mystérion*, 'mystery, secret'. Old English *rūn*, Old Norse *rún* and Old High-German *rūna* can also mean whispered, secret or private counsel. This association with secrets and religious mysteries has been used to promote the popular belief that runic characters have an inherently magical or mystical significance. However, there is evidence that *rūn-* 'rune' may actually (and more prosaically) be related to verbs meaning 'dig', 'carve', 'scratch', as are words for writing in many other languages (such as the Greek word *graphein*, which means 'to paint').

Interpreting the inscriptions

The first step in deciphering an inscription is to read it – that is, to identify the characters which are present – and this can be a frustrating exercise. If the object is worn, corroded or damaged, runes may not be legible, and deliberate carvings may be difficult to distinguish from unintentional scratches. Many objects are marked with shapes or symbols which are labelled 'rune-like' or 'runic', but which do not represent writing, and so these can be misleading. (The many difficulties posed by the script are discussed in greater detail in chapter 5.)

Assuming we can identify the marks on an object as runic characters, the next task is to try and make sense of the inscription as a piece of language – in other words, to produce one or more interpretations. In order to do this, we need to gather as much informtion as possible about the type of object, the material from which it is made, the techniques used for carving the runes, the relationship of the inscription to decoration and other elements of design, and the archaeological context in which the object was found. All of these factors can help us to understand what might have been written on it, by whom, and why. Modern archaeology places a great deal of emphasis on the context of a find: the circumstances in which the object was deposited can provide us with useful information about its history – and the history of the people who made, owned and used it. In fact, the overall layout of a site and its position in the local landscape can be at least as informative as the objects that are recovered from an excavation.

That said, the object itself, of course, is a vital source of information, even when we do not have an archaeological context. Techniques of manufacture and styles of decoration can be used to identify, or at least give an indication of, when and where an object was made. Accompanying imagery and decoration can also be revealing in terms of context and may help us to understand the text.

The type of material and the quality of workmanship can also hint at the status of the person for whom an object was made. We can also examine it for signs of wear and tear to learn about its history: items worn next to clothing – such as jewellery, dress accessories or scabbard (sword-sheath) fittings – will become worn and scratched over time, so if one of these items has seen long use, we may be able to see the physical signs.

About this book

Since runes were mainly used for carving, rather than for writing manuscripts, this book will focus on examples of inscribed objects to illustrate the use of runic script. The British Museum's rich collection contains many inscribed objects found in the British Isles, to which we will give particular attention alongside finds from Scandinavia and elsewhere. By analysing the texts found on these objects we will trace the origins of the runic script, its development over the centuries during which it was used and how it has been interpreted and used in more recent times. By doing so the book will help us better understand the lives of people who inhabited Europe over a thousand years ago, and reveal what runes meant to them as well as what they have meant to modern generations. For a more detailed survey of known inscriptions, you might like to refer to some of the longer texts in the Further reading section (pp. 102–105).

Reading and interpreting inscriptions is rarely a straightforward matter. Inscribed objects may be so badly worn or corroded that the characters are difficult to read, and even when we can read them, it can be difficult to work out what they meant to the people who made them. For some of the inscriptions we will be looking at, scholars have proposed dozens of possible interpretations, although not all inscriptions are so controversial. Chapter 5 will look in closer detail at the problems runologists face when trying to understand runes.

Transliteration and phonetic transcription

This book will use some of the same conventions that academics use when discussing runic inscriptions. Rather than writing out a text in runes, it is normal to transliterate the characters using their nearest Roman-letter equivalents in bold type (e.g., **horna** for the runes ᚺᛜᚱᚾᚨ). When Roman letters and runes appear in the same inscription, the Roman letters are written as capitals. Where the identification of a character is uncertain (for example, when wear or damage has obscured the carvings), we will place it in parentheses in the transliteration, e.g., (**f**).

Carvers sometimes combine two (or occasionally three) runes into what is known as a 'bindrune'. When translating runic inscriptions, bindrunes are marked with a breve over the letters: for example, the bindrune on the Undley bracteate (a gold pendant featured shortly), which combines ᚷ and ᚨ, will be transliterated **ga͡ or gæ͡** (see pp. 26–7).

The transliteration of runic characters helps us to read and compare written forms, but we sometimes need to look more carefully at the relationship between the written character and the sound, or the sound which it represents. For this purpose, symbols from the International Phonetic Alphabet (IPA) will be used. IPA characters will be placed between square brackets, e.g., [a]. Below is a list of the characters used in the book, with a note on pronunciation where necessary. For more information, you may want to consult the International Phonetic Association's website: <http://www.langsci.ucl.ac.uk/ipa/>.

[a]	The vowel of modern German *mann*.
[ã]	A 'nasalized' [a]-sound, a bit like the vowel in French *main*.
[æ]	The vowel of modern English *cat*.
[ɑ]	The vowel of modern (British) English *car*, but short.
[b]	
[ç]	The *ch* sound of German *ich*.
[d]	
[ð]	The 'voiced' *th* of modern English *this*.
[e]	A 'close' *e*-sound like that of French *été*, rather than the more open sound of English *hen* (which is normally transcribed [ɛ]).
[f]	
[g]	Pronounced 'hard', as in modern English *good*.
[h]	
[i]	The vowel of modern English *see*, but short; compare modern French *il*.
[j]	The *y* sound of modern English *yet*.
[k]	Pronounced 'hard', as in modern English *cat*.

[l]

[m]

[n]

[ŋ]   The *ng* sound of modern standard English *long*.

[o]   The vowel of modern American English *go*, but
        short; compare French *eau*.

[œ]   The vowel of modern German *Mönch*, or
        French *œuf*.

[p]

[r]   Strictly speaking, this symbol represents a 'trilled'
        r, as in modern Italian. In practice, it is often used
        for other *r*-sounds as well.

[s]

[ʃ]   The sound of *sh* in modern English *shell*.

[t]

[tʃ]   The sound of *ch* in modern English *church*.

[θ]   The 'voiceless' *th* of modern English *thin*. Some
        authors use the character *þ* ('thorn'), which is
        based on the rune ᚦ, in phonetic transcriptions;
        but it is not an IPA character and will be avoided
        in this book.

[u]   The vowel of modern English *who*, but short;
        compare French *ou*.

[v]

[w]

[x]   The *ch* sound of Scots *loch*, or modern German
        ach; not the *ks* sound.

[y]   The vowel of modern French *tu*.

[z]   As in modern English *zoo*, not *ts* as in German
        and some other languages.

When a vowel is long, it is followed by the mark : (e.g.,
modern British English *car* would be transcribed [kɑ:]).

CHAPTER ONE

The origin of runic writing

We do not know the exact circumstances of the origin of runic writing and so we must infer what we can from the available evidence. The earliest surviving inscriptions date from the mid to late second century AD. An earlier first-century brooch found at Meldorf in northern Germany bears an inscription in characters that can be read as either runes or Roman letters, but there is some controversy over which was intended. Whether the Meldorf inscription is runic or not, it is generally believed that the script is significantly older than the earliest known inscriptions and originates between *c.*500 BC and *c.*AD 100.

The earliest finds are concentrated in southern Scandinavia, which might imply that runes have their origins somewhere in this region, perhaps in Denmark. However, almost all of these inscriptions are on portable objects, and since we know from the archaeological record that peoples in ancient Europe had extensive networks of trade and exchange, we cannot assume that a particular object was made or inscribed near to where it was deposited. In fact the concentration of finds in Denmark may be an accident of preservation: it is in this region that there seems to have been a practice of deliberately depositing objects (chiefly weaponry and war gear) in bogs. The bog deposits, which may have had a religious function, are of great archaeological value because the conditions are favourable for the preservation not only of metal, but of perishable materials such as wood.

The most hotly debated issue surrounding the origin of runes is the question of their connections with other writing systems. There can be little doubt that runes are adapted from one Mediterranean alphabet or another: many of the characters bear a formal resemblance to Greek and/or Roman letters with similar sound-values (compare, for example, ⟨, Roman S and Greek Σ). Arguably closer correspondences can be found with letters from other alphabets used in Italy or in the Alpine region, and in the mid twentieth century the favoured theory was that runes were originally modelled on one or more of these 'North Italic' alphabets. More recently, the Greek and Roman models have gained support, and a possible connection with the Phoenician alphabet has been proposed (the ancient region of Phoenicia was situated on the modern Lebanese coast, with adjoining parts to modern Syria and Israel), based on the parallels between the Phoenician letter-names (*alf* 'ox', *bet* 'house', *gaml* 'camel', etc) and the rune-names (see chapter 4). The Roman hypothesis is currently the preferred one, but the problem is unlikely ever to be solved with any certainty. However, one point to emphasize is that all of these theories reflect substantial contact with cultures in the wider Mediterranean world. It is tempting to think of Scandinavia and neighbouring regions as a remote, isolated area inhabited by a people apart from the 'civilized' world, but in reality, the peoples of northern Europe were part of an extensive network which traded in a variety of goods, as well as aspects of culture – including writing.

The runic alphabet

Runes are arranged in a conventional order very different from that of the Mediterranean alphabets, and it has become the norm to refer to the runic alphabets as *futharks*, from the values of the first six runes f u þ a r k. (The letter þ 'thorn', is a modified rune which stands for the 'th' sound [ɵ]. Medieval English scribes used this letter (see pp. 38–9), and it is still used in the modern Icelandic spelling.) The earliest of these alphabets, containing twenty-four letters, is known as the Older Futhark.

In total, around 400 inscriptions using Older Futhark runes are known. They span a period from the second to the seventh century AD, and appear on a wide range of objects including weapons, tools, jewellery, belt fittings and a small number of stones. The bulk of the material originates from Scandinavia, but there is a significant cluster of finds in southern Germany, and occasional examples appear in other parts of Europe, too.

Fig. 2 Limestone slab from a grave site at Kylver in Gotland, Sweden. Inscribed on the stone is a complete futhark, one of just four early examples. Probably 5th century. H. 105 cm; W. 75 cm. National Historical Museum, Stockholm.

There are just four early inscriptions containing complete or near-complete futharks – precious examples of the first runic alphabets. Probably the earliest of them is on a limestone slab from a grave site at Kylver in Gotland, Sweden (fig. 2), conventionally (though uncertainly) dated to the fifth century. On page 18 is a list of the Kylver runes (in a standardized form). Three of the characters (**a s b**) are reversed, which is quite common in early inscriptions.

The Kylver stone also has some other carvings: immediately after the futhark is a symbol resembling a fir-tree, and to the right of this is a sequence of runes **sueus**. The functions of these carvings are unknown: it has been proposed that the futhark and these other markings might have served some magical purpose (such as to prevent the dead person walking out of the grave). On the other hand, it is also possible that the inscription was made at an earlier date for some other purpose, and then reused in the grave construction. Although one of the common uses of runic writing (especially in Viking-Age Scandinavia – see chapter 3) was for memorializing the dead, there are no other known examples of runic inscriptions placed inside burial chambers.

The Kylver inscription in particular gives us no explicit information about what it is for, so we must be extremely cautious in trying to interpret it.

Inscriptions in the Older Futhark

Older Futhark inscriptions are often short and difficult to interpret, but they can tell us something about the people who made, owned or used them even if the information can be hard to recover. Personal names – in many cases probably those of the object's maker or owner – are especially common. Some inscriptions seem to be connected with gift-giving: for example, a disc-brooch from a sixth-century woman's grave at Bad Krozingen in Baden-Württemberg,

Rune	Transliteration	Sound value
ᚠ	**f**	[f]
ᚢ	**u**	[u]
ᚦ	**þ**	[θ]
ᚨ	**a**	[a]
ᚱ	**r**	[r]
ᚲ	**k**	[k]
ᚷ	**g**	[g]
ᚹ	**w**	[w]
ᚺ	**h**	[h]
ᚾ	**n**	[n]
ᛁ	**i**	[i]
ᛃ	**j**	[j]
ᛈ	**p**	[p]
ᛇ	**ï** (or sometimes **æ, ɨ** or **ė**).	Where used, it usually represents [i]. Its original sound-value is uncertain.
ᛉ	**z** (some authors use **R**).	[z], or possibly an [r]-like sound.
ᛋ	**s**	[s]
ᛏ	**t**	[t]
ᛒ	**b**	[b]
ᛖ	**e**	[e]
ᛗ	**m**	[m]
ᛚ	**l**	[l]
ᛜ	**ŋ**	[ŋ] or [ŋg] or [iŋg]
ᛞ	**d**	[d]
ᛟ	**o**	[o]

south-west Germany, has the text **boba:leub agirike**
'Boba [is] dear to Agirik' (Boba being a woman's name
– perhaps, but not necessarily, that of the woman in the
grave – and Agirik a man's name). The brooch seems to
have been given as a token of personal affection, although
we have no way of knowing who these two people were or
what the relationship between them was. Boba and Agirik
might have been husband and wife, or relatives, or lord
and valued servant.

Sometimes we are fortunate enough to find a longer,
more intelligible text. A fine example was inscribed on a
(probably) fifth-century gold drinking-horn, one of a pair
discovered at Gallehus in Jutland, Denmark in 1734.
Unfortunately, both horns were stolen and melted down in
1802, so we know of them only from drawings. The horns
in the British Museum's collection (fig. 3 and overleaf) are
copied from a pair of nineteenth-century replicas based on
these drawings. The inscription reads: **ekhlewagastiz:
holtijaz:horna:tawido** 'I, Hlewagastiz, [a son?

Fig. 3 and *overleaf*
Detail and full view of
the British Museum
copies of the Gallehus
drinking-horns. The
original horns were
created in gold in
(probably) the 5th
century. L. 52.5 cm.
British Museum
1885,OA.160.a and
16l.a.

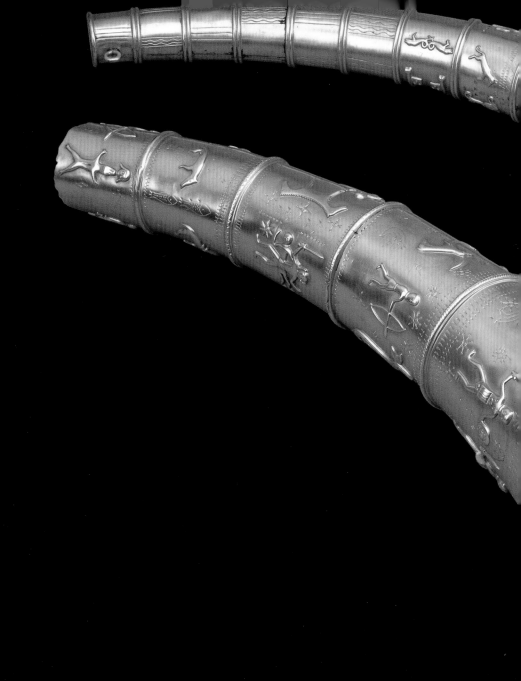

descendant? follower?] of Holt, made the horn[s?]'. In this short verse, the named individual identifies himself clearly as the maker of the inscribed object, and identifies himself by his social position as a member of a family, clan, tribe or other social group. It is unfortunate that we have no more information about the circumstances of the find, so we do not know what happened to the horns between their manufacture and their discovery; but the horns represent a considerable quantity of gold (both are over 50 cm in length) and fine craftsmanship, displaying the wealth and influence of whoever commissioned them. This kind of ostentatious display seems to have been an important part of northern European politics in this period: lords advertised their strength by showing off their wealth, and distributing it among their followers.

Another practice that we find among the early inscriptions (and in later traditions as well) is that of naming the inscribed object or material. Combs that say 'comb' seem to be quite popular: the earliest example is from the third century, and was found at Frienstedt in northern Germany. Several similarly inscribed combs have been found, with dates ranging from the eighth to the tenth centuries (one of these is pictured on pp. 60–1). Another of the early inscriptions from Germany is on a footstool from a fifth-century grave near Wremen in Lower Saxony. The inscription contains the sequence **ksamella**, which appears to be a borrowed form of the Latin *scamella* 'step, footstool', with the first two characters transposed.

Many Older Futhark inscriptions are unintelligible to the modern reader, even when they are quite clearly legible. Some seem to be nothing more than a meaningless jumble of characters and may not say anything at all. Others contain what appears to be meaningful text, but cannot be interpreted satisfactorily. One example of this type is a silver-gilt brooch from the British Museum (fig. 4).

The brooch is of a recognized type known from sixth-century burials in Alamannia (a region now in southern

Fig. 4 Silver-gilt brooch with garnet. Alamannia (now in southern Germany), 6th century. L. 7.4 cm. British Museum 1893,0618.32. Acquired from the collection of Thomas Bateman.

Germany), although it was reported as having been found in Kent, England so it may have been an import. The inscription on the back of the brooch is in three lines, one of them written much larger than the others. The marks are fairly easy to see, but they make little sense. One possible reading (although by no means the only one) would be **gamu** or **gadu** (for the top row), **iku** (for the larger characters), and perhaps **wifa** for the bottom row. **Wifa** might represent *wīfa* 'women's', but this is uncertain, and even if it is correct, the sense of the whole inscription remains obscure.

The possibility of reading the words of people who lived many centuries ago is what makes the study of these inscriptions so exciting, but it can be very frustrating to the modern observer when what is written appears to make no sense. Somebody put these marks on the brooch, and he or she must have had a reason for doing so; yet we cannot tell what that reason was. We will look again at this issue in chapter 5.

CHAPTER TWO

From futhark to futhorc: Anglo-Saxon runes

The seventh century is something of a turning point in the history of runic writing. In Scandinavia, this period saw the beginning of the process which led to the establishment of new futharks (alphabets) with fewer letters and simpler letter-forms (see Chapter 3). In Britain, meanwhile, the futhark was expanded to twenty-eight letters or more. This reformed futhark (or *futhorc*) was established by the end of the seventh century, but has its roots in some adaptations of the writing system which began much earlier.

The traditional story of the Anglo-Saxon settlement of Britain, popularized by the Northumbrian scholar Bede in the early eighth century, is familiar to many of us. According to this narrative, the Roman province of Britain was left vulnerable to attack following the withdrawal of troops in the early fifth century. In AD 449, the British ruler Vortigern hired mercenaries led by the brothers Hengist and Horsa to help him fight off raiders from the north.

The mercenaries were given land in the east of the island in exchange for their service; but they soon rebelled, slaughtering or driving out the Britons and occupying the land. Bede writes that the invaders were from three groups: Angles (from the region known as Angeln, in the area where the Jutland peninsula joins what is now northern Germany), Saxons (from further west on the North Sea coast of Germany) and Jutes (from Jutland).[1]

This narrative may contain some elements of historical truth, but it is little more than a myth. What has become clear thanks to the work of archaeologists and historians in recent decades is that the story of the 'Anglo-Saxon' invaders entirely sweeping away the existing population is at best an exaggeration. Over the course of the fifth and sixth centuries there was an emergence of new elites, particularly in eastern and south-eastern areas; but agricultural practice and territorial divisions in Britain seem (to some extent, at least) to continue from the Roman period. There is an ongoing debate about the scale of migration, and about whether or not we should see the process as one of large-scale invasion or more gradual settlement. What we do know is that artefacts from this period which are found in Britain show strong influence from the cultures of Scandinavia, Frisia[2] and the territory of the Franks (covering large parts of modern France and western Germany). Another important aspect of culture which came to Britain with migrants, of course, was language: the Germanic dialects of the early settlers formed what eventually became English. As well as their speech, it seems that at least some of these settlers brought with them their knowledge of runic writing.

The early runic inscriptions of Britain and Frisia use a slightly expanded set of runes. The dialects spoken in these areas had a more complex vowel system than the language of the earliest inscriptions, which used the Older Futhark (see chapter 1), so to represent their speech more effectively,

carvers created two new runes – both modified forms of ᚠ
– and some of the older characters developed new sound-
values:

Rune:	ᚠ	ᚪ	ᚫ		ᛟ
Transliteration:	**æ**	**a**	**ã** (later **o**)		**œ**
Sound:	[æ]	[ɑ]	[ɑ̃] (later [o])		[œ][3]

The new runes can be seen on some of the earliest
rune-inscribed objects found in Britain. One of the most
intriguing of these is a gold bracteate found at Undley in
Suffolk, England in 1981 (fig. 5).

Bracteates are ornaments or pendants, usually made of
gold, which originated as imitations of Roman medallions
and coins. They seem to have been popular in some parts
of northern Europe between c.AD 450–550: hundreds of
examples have been found in Denmark, with smaller
numbers in Norway, Sweden and Continental Europe,
and a handful of finds in England.

The Undley bracteate is of a relatively early type. Some
aspects of the design suggest that it may have been made
in northern Germany or southern Denmark and either
brought to England by an early settler, or imported through
trade. However, runic inscriptions from the Continental
region in question are very scarce, and none of them use
the additional 'Anglo-Frisian' runes, which the Undley
bracteate does. In consideration of these facts and some
peculiarities of the design – such as the motif of the wolf
and twins, adapted from the image of Romulus and Remus
(the mythical founders of Rome, abandoned as babies
and suckled by a she-wolf) on some Roman coins, but
unparalleled on other bracteates – some runologists have
argued that the Undley bracteate might have been made
in England. The story of Romulus and Remus (or perhaps
some locally adapted version of it) seems to have had an

Fig. 5 The Undley bracteate, with profile of a head, wolf with Romulus and Remus, and runic inscription. Germanic, 5th century. Diam. 2.3 cm. British Museum 1984,1101.1.

enduring appeal in Anglo-Saxon England. Most famously, it is the subject of one of the side panels on the Franks Casket (see pp. 48–9).

The helmeted and bearded male bust in the centre of the bracteate is another aspect of the design which is clearly inspired by Roman coins. Many early bracteates have similar heads, and later types elaborated on this design. Some of them have a whole human figure, often accompanied by animals; the most common bracteate type depicts a male head above a horse. The thematic developments of bracteate design have led to speculation that the human figure represents a god (perhaps Wodan/Óðinn, the chief of the gods in medieval Norse mythology), but there is little evidence to support this.

The inscription is quite easy to read, but difficult to interpret. From right to left, it reads: **gǣgōgǣ·mægæ· medu** (the small circles are word-division marks). **mægæ·medu** is commonly believed to represent an early form of *maga mēd*, 'kinsmen's reward' or *mæge mēd* 'reward for [a/the] kinsman', which would fit with the theory that bracteates may have been used as tokens of esteem or status, given to warriors in recognition of their military service. Other interpretations have been proposed (**medu** could, for instance, represent Old English *medu* 'mead').

The series of bindrunes is more problematic. They may be abbreviations (perhaps standing for the rune-names – see chapter 4), or the whole sequence might represent a

Fig. 6 Runic inscription on the back of a scabbard mount (sword sheath) from a 6th-century grave at Chessell Down on the Isle of Wight. Silver, Anglo-Saxon, 5th–6th century. L. 5.5 cm. British Museum 1867,0729.150.

single word. The most popular interpretation is that proposed by Bengt Odenstedt, who suggested that **gǣgōgǣ** represents a word *gǣgōjǣ* 'howler', referring to the wolf depicted on the bracteate. The controversies about the bracteate's provenance and the meaning of the inscription have not yet been resolved. For a more detailed discussion, see Parsons (1999: 62–7).

Another very early example of the new rune ᛇ is on a scabbard mount (sword sheath) from a sixth-century grave at Chessell Down on the Isle of Wight (fig. 6). (For more information about the Chessell Down cemetery, see p. 86.)

The inscription reads **æko:?œri** (with ᚩ possibly standing for its new sound [œ]), but has not been satisfactorily interpreted. **æko** might be a personal name. The rune following the division-mark, ᚲ, resembles the normal form of **k** in Viking Age and medieval Scandinavia (chapter 3), but this is a later development. ᚲ could be a rare form of **s**, known from other Anglo-Saxon inscriptions; or it could be a damaged or poorly carved form of another rune such as ᚠ, ᚹ or ᚦ.

The earliest example of ᚠ is on a gold coin (fig. 7), probably minted in Frisia in the late sixth century. The inscription is usually transliterated **skanomodu**, which may represent a personal name. It has the new **a**-rune ᚠ, but it uses ᚩ in a position where it must have its older sound value [o] or [oː], not the new value [œ]. Often, names in early coin inscriptions are those of moneyers (the individuals responsible for organizing the issue of coins) rather than of the kings and archbishops under whose authority the coins were issued.

Perhaps the earliest English inscription containing ᚠ is on one of a pair of gold fragments (possibly from a finger-ring) found on the beach near Selsey in West Sussex (fig. 8).

ᚠ is quite clearly legible, although it is not very helpful to the modern scholar because the inscription as a whole is unintelligible (a reading **brnrn anmu** has been proposed,

Fig. 7 Reverse of gold coin. The runic inscription surrounds a standing figure in military costume, holding a standard and a little Victory. His left foot is trampling a fallen captive. Probably Frisia, late 6th century. British Museum Keary.1. Donated by King George III.

but this cannot be rendered into meaningful language). The dating of the object is also very uncertain, but it may be as early as the seventh century. A number of later Anglo-Saxon finger-rings carry runic (or mixed runic and Roman) inscriptions that seem to be magical charms, perhaps to protect against bleeding (see pp. 84–5); while others record the names of makers and/or owners (an example is discussed on p. 38). If the Selsey fragments were originally part of a ring, then the inscription might have belonged to one of these two types, but we cannot be sure.

All of these early examples are important and

Fig. 8 Pair of gold fragments, possibly from a finger-ring. England, Anglo-Saxon, 5th–11th centuries. L. 1.9 cm. British Museum 1878,0315.4. Donated by Henry Willet.

interesting as early evidence for the changes in the writing system, yet they present difficulties of interpretation which involve some rather technical arguments about phonology (the study of the script's sound system). We will not go into them here, but they do highlight some of the difficulties runologists face in interpreting inscriptions. These issues will be discussed further in chapter 5.

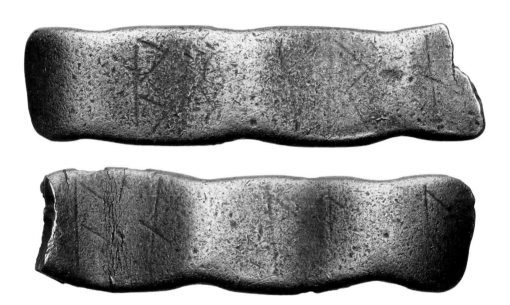

Other early inscriptions

In total, there are some 40–50 inscriptions in England dated before c.AD 700 (although in some cases, the dates are very uncertain). Some are illegible, and many of those we can read are difficult to interpret – as we have seen with the early witnesses to the new runes. Following are a few more examples from the early period that emphasize this point.

A disc brooch from a late sixth or early seventh century grave at Buckland, near Dover, England has an inscription

Fig. 9 Back of a silver disc brooch with a confusing inscription of Old English runes. Anglo-Saxon, late 6th or early 7th century. Diam. 4.2 cm. British Museum 1963,1108. 583. Purchased with contribution from the Trustees of the Christy Fund.

on the back which defies interpretation (fig. 9). It consists of two groups of characters: (A) **bl(n)??b**; (B) **iwd**. The uncertain rune here is the form ᛈ, which we saw on the Chessell Down scabbard mount (fig. 7). If this represents **s**, then part of the first group might be a slightly garbled form of the Old English word *bliss* 'bliss, joy', but this is very uncertain. No one has proposed any interpretation of the second group. A characteristic feature of the use of runes in Germany is the scratching of short inscriptions, such as this, onto the backs of brooches (see p. 19 for an early example). The Dover brooch was made in England, but the inscription may reflect the intensive cultural contacts between Kent and the expanding Frankish empire in the sixth and seventh centuries.

By the end of the seventh century, some of the emerging Anglo-Saxon kingdoms had started producing their own coins, some with runic legends. Several coin issues of the late seventh century use runes to record the names of moneyers, such as **æpa** and **pada**. Some earlier issues carry incomprehensible and possibly meaningless sequences of runes.

This early coin (fig. 10) is part of a group usually dated *c*.AD 620–40. The legend reads **benu:tigoii**. Other coins

Fig. 10 Reverse of gold coin with runic inscription arranged around a cross on three steps. England, *c*.AD 620–40. British Museum 1869, 0404.1. Donated by T.S. Bazley, Esq.

Fig. 11 Carved *astragalus* (ankle-bone) of a roe-deer, found in a cremation burial in Norfolk, England, dating to the 5th century. Norwich Castle Museum and Art Gallery.

in the same group use the spelling **benu:+:tidi**, which is equally unintelligible.

Luckily, not all early Anglo-Saxon inscriptions are so problematic. One of the earliest (fig. 11) is clearly legible and can be interpreted with confidence.

It is carved into the *astragalus* (ankle-bone) of a roe-deer, found in a fifth-century cremation burial at Caistor-by-Norwich in Norfolk, England. The inscription reads **raïhan** (with the older **a**-rune, ᚨ), which probably means 'roe-deer's [bone]'; but the word 'roe-deer' could also be a man's name, so the inscription would mean 'Raiha's [bone]'. This is another example where an inscription has been used to indicate belonging. The urn in which this item was found contained 35 other *astragali*, mainly of sheep, and 33 flat bone pieces. This collection of objects may have been a set of gaming pieces.

The Anglo-Saxon futhorc

Several more runes were added to the runic alphabet during the seventh and eighth centuries, producing an expanded futhark which we call the *futhorc*, as the new **o**-rune ᚩ was moved into the fourth position. Most inscriptions use an inventory of twenty-eight runes. Here is a standard version:

No.	Rune	Transliteration	Comments on sound-value
1	ᚠ	**f**	
2	ᚢ	**u**	
3	ᚦ	**þ**	
4	ᚩ	**o**	
5	ᚱ	**r**	
6	ᚳ	**c**	Before i, e or y, this is usually pronounced something like [tʃ] (as in modern English *church*, Old English *cyrice*).
7	ᚷ	**g**	Before i or e, this is pronounced something like [j] (as in modern English *yellow*, Old English *geolu*).
8	ᚹ	**w**	
9	ᚺ	**h**	
10	ᚾ	**n**	
11	ᛁ	**i**	
12	ᛄ	**j**	
13	ᛇ	**ï / i / ė / ç / ʒ**	On the rare occasions when this rune appears, it usually represents [i]. In a few places, it is used for the consonants [ç] or [x].

No.	Rune	Transliteration	Comments on sound-value
14	ᛈ	**p**	
15	ᛉ	**x**	The older [z]-sound was no longer used in Old English, and this rune was given a new value, [ks] or [xs].
16	ᛋ	**s**	
17	ᛏ	**t**	
18	ᛒ	**b**	
19	ᛖ	**e**	
20	ᛗ	**m**	
21	ᛚ	**l**	
22	ᛝ	**ŋ / ng**	
23	ᛞ	**d**	
24	ᛟ	**œ**	
25	ᚪ	**a**	
26	ᚨ	**æ**	
27	ᚣ	**y**	
28	ᛠ	**ea**	This is a diphthong pronounced like [æ] + [ɑ] (rather difficult for a modern English speaker).
A few Northumbrian inscriptions use one or more extra runes:			
29	ᚸ	**ḡ**	[g] (distinguished from the [j]-sound of g).
30	ᚲ	**k**	[k] (distinguished from the [tʃ]-like sound of c).
31	ᛤ	**k̄**	[k] where it occurs before i, e, y (where we would normally get the [tʃ]-sound of c), as in *cyning* 'king'.

Fig. 12 Detail of an iron sword. Anglo-Saxon, c.10th century. L. (overall) 72.1 cm. British Museum 1857,0623.1.

The order and (to an extent) the forms of the runes in the futhorc were well established by the end of the seventh century, probably as a result of deliberate reform by church scholars. Variations do still appear, though. A tenth-century *seax* (single-edged short sword) found in the River Thames near Battersea, in London (fig. 12) has an inlaid runic inscription consisting of a futhorc and the name **beagnoþ**, which may be the name of the maker or the owner.

This inscription is interesting because it is the only complete futhorc preserved in an inscription, rather than in a scholarly manuscript (see p. 54), and because it uses several unusual variant forms: + for **j**, ᛤ for **y** and ᛢ for **œ**. The order of the runes also differs slightly from the 'standardized' futhorc given on pp. 35–36. These variations might indicate that the craftsman who made the object was unfamiliar with runic writing, or they may reflect genuine differences of arrangement and form. The unusual œ-rune is certainly found elsewhere, albeit rarely. We cannot say for sure what the purpose of this inscription was, but finely inlaid weapons such as this may have been intended for display or for some sort of ceremonial purpose, rather than for fighting, as we might assume.

The majority of Anglo-Saxon inscriptions use the twenty-eight-letter futhorc; the additional Northumbrian runes (the last three in the table on p. 36) are quite rare. Some manuscript sources record additional characters such as ᛥ (*stān*) and ᛣ (*cweorth*), but there is no evidence that these were ever used epigraphically, that is, in inscriptions.

Runes and the Roman alphabet

The seventh century was a period of dramatic social, political and economic changes in the Anglo-Saxon kingdoms. The adoption of Christianity required the establishment of religious communities and the encouragement of Latin literacy, but this did not mean that people abandoned their other writing system. If anything, the spread of literacy in religious communities seems to have encouraged the reform of the futhorc and a growth in the use of runes for writing the vernacular, particularly in Northumbria (see p. 41).

Both runic and Roman characters were used for carving on stone monuments and portable objects, and it is not unusual to find both scripts on the same object (as on the back of the Franks Casket – see pp. 44–54). Sometimes we find inscriptions which mix runes and Roman letters together. A good example of a mixed-script text is on a ninth-century gold ring found in Manchester (fig. 13).

With the words separated out, it reads **æDRED MEC AH EAnRED MEC agROf** 'Ædred owns me, Eanred engraved me'. The carver seems to have selected freely from both alphabets: for example, both Roman A and runic **a** are used to write [ɑː] in AH 'owns' and **agROf** 'engraved'.

For writing manuscripts, only Roman script was used, with certain modifications, including the adoption of two runes as additional letters. Early Anglo-Saxon scribes,

Fig. 13 Runic inscribed gold finger-ring. Late Anglo-Saxon, 9th century. Found in Manchester, England. Diam. 2.3 cm. British Museum SLRings.64. Bequeathed by Sir Hans Sloane.

probably following the practice of their Irish contemporaries, used the letters *th* to spell [θ] and [ð], but this spelling was gradually replaced by an adapted form of the rune Þ (the letter 'thorn'), which remained in use in English manuscripts for centuries after the Norman Conquest in the eleventh century. A rounded form of Ƿ ('wynn') was also adopted for [w], another sound for which the Roman alphabet did not have a letter (Roman V originally served this purpose but it was pronounced [v] in late imperial and medieval Latin). We can see these adaptations in Roman-alphabet inscriptions as well as in manuscripts: an eleventh-century disc brooch found at Sutton in Cambridgeshire, England (fig. 14), has an inscription on the back which is in Roman capitals, but uses Ƿ for [w] (in a form more like that used in manuscripts than that of earlier runic inscriptions). It does not, however, use Þ for [θ] / [ð]; instead, it uses Ð ('eth', a modified Roman D).

The inscription reads ÆDVƿEN ME AG AGE HYO DRIHTEN DRIHTEN HINE AƿERIE ÐE ME HIRE ÆTFERIE BVTON HYO ME SELLE HIRE AGENES ƿILLES, 'Æðwynn [or Eadwynn] owns me, may the Lord own her. May the Lord curse him who takes me from her, unless she gives me voluntarily' (text and translation from Okasha 1971, no. 114). The use of the letter Ƿ does not reflect a mixing of scripts so much as the integration of an originally runic character into the English version of the Roman alphabet.

Several Old English riddles contain words written in runes that give a clue to the riddle's solution. More sophisticated are the poems written by (or ascribed to) Cynewulf, in which the Anglo-Saxon poet's name is spelled out in runes incorporated into the text. All of these practices point to a perception of runes as something rather exotic and even secret, suitable for codes, riddles and word-play.

You can find more information about manuscript runes in Derolez (1954) and in Page (1999), chapter 5.

Northumbria and the spread of literacy

Over the course of the seventh and eighth centuries Northumbria became not only one of the most powerful Anglo-Saxon kingdoms, but also a centre of religion and learning and one that proved instrumental in the spread of literacy. The monastic communities of this northern-England kingdom created stone monuments with elaborate decorations, and religious inscriptions using both Roman and runic script. Several stone crosses survive from Northumbria; two of the earliest, largest and most impressive of Anglo-Saxon inscriptions are those at Bewcastle in Cumbria and Ruthwell in Dumfries and Galloway, both probably dating from the early eighth century. The Ruthwell inscription contains a version of a poem about the Crucifixion, told in the first person from the point of view of the Cross. A longer version of this poem – known to modern readers as the *Dream of the Rood* – is recorded in a late tenth-century manuscript which now belongs to the Biblioteca Capitolare at Vercelli, Italy. The inscription on the Bewcastle cross is now barely legible, but it contains a woman's name, Cyniburh (**kynibur?g̅**) and the name of Christ (**g(e)ssus | kristtus**). Both crosses were carved with intricate decorative motifs and religious imagery, and they are outstanding examples of Northumbrian craftsmanship and skill in runic writing, using an expanded set of runes to mark some quite subtle differences in the spoken language (see p. 36). Far from being associated with pagan magic, as is sometimes claimed, the high point of runic literacy in England was in Northumbria's religious communities.

The other Northumbrian stone monuments are less grand, and their inscriptions are for the most part simple memorials, sometimes just recording the name of the deceased. The British Museum has two fragments of stone crosses with surviving runic inscriptions: one from Monkwearmouth, Tyne and Wear, and one from Lancaster.

Fig. 14 Silver disc-brooch found at Sutton in Cambridgeshire, England. On the back of the brooch (above) is an inscription in Roman capitals. 11th century. Diam. 14.9 cm. British Museum 1951,1011.1.

Fig. 15 Stone cross fragment from Monkwearmouth, Tyne and Wear. 10th or 11th century. H. 31.4 cm. British Museum 1880,0313.1.

Fig. 16 *Right* (detail) and *opposite* The remains of the stone monumental cross known as the Lancaster Cross. One arm is missing. Lancaster, late 9th century. H. 9.2 cm. British Museum 1868,1004.3. Donated by Natural History Society of Manchester.

The Monkwearmouth inscription (fig. 15) from
the tenth/eleventh century is simple in both style and
content, consisting just of a man's name, **tidfirþ**.

The Lancaster fragment (fig. 16) which dates to
the late ninth century has, in contrast, fine interlaced
decoration and a fairly well preserved inscription:
gibidæþforæcynibalþcuþbere… 'Pray for Cynibalþ.
Cuþbere–.' The second name, which may be a form
of Cuthbert, probably belongs to the person who
commissioned the monument.

The Franks Casket

One of the finest examples of Anglo-Saxon craftsmanship
and runic writing is the whalebone casket donated to the
British Museum by Sir Augustus Wollaston Franks in 1867.
It was probably made in Northumbria in the early eighth
century. Its intended function is not known, but it might
have been used as a reliquary. The right-hand panel was
separated from the rest of the casket at some point, and
is now in the Museo Nazionale del Bargello in Florence,
Italy. A cast of this panel has been fitted to the casket at
the British Museum.

The casket is elaborately carved with images from
Christian, classical Roman and secular traditions.
Inscriptions, which are mostly written in the futhorc and
Old English, run around the borders of the front, back
and sides (parts of the lid are missing, so we do not know
whether or not this originally had a border inscription).
There are also runic 'captions' embedded in the pictorial
scenes. Much controversy surrounds the interpretation of
the images and some of the inscriptions; sadly, we do not
have space here to discuss it in full detail, so an overview
is given. For more information, see Page (1999: 172–9)
and Webster (1999; 2012).

The front panel (fig. 17 and overleaf) is divided into

Fig. 17 and *overleaf*
The front panel of the
Franks Casket.
Whalebone, probably
Northumbria, England,
early 8th century.
L. 23 cm; D. 19 cm;
H. 13 cm. British
Museum 1867,
0120.1. Donated by
Sir Augustus
Wollaston Franks.

two parts. On the right are the Magi (the three kings) visiting Christ (with the label **mægi** 'Magi'). The left part depicts the story of Weland, versions of which are recorded in medieval Scandinavian sources. The smith Weland (or Vǫlundr in Old Norse) is captured by the king Niðuðr. The king has him hamstrung so that he cannot escape, but Vǫlundr exacts a violent revenge: he murders Niðuðr's sons, rapes his daughter and (in one version of the story) flees on wings made from the feathers of birds caught by his brother Egil, a skilled archer.

The border inscription on the front contains a poem about the whale from whose bone the casket is made. Reading clockwise from the top left-hand corner, it reads:

fisc·flodu· | ahofonferg | enberig | warþga:sricgror nþærheongreutgiswom | hronæsban.

Fig. 18 The lid of the casket.

We can render this into Old English as follows:

Fisc flōdu ahōf on fergenberig. Warþ gāsric grorn, þǣr he on greut giswom. Hronæs bān.

Page (see reference above) translated this text as:
'The fish beat up the sea onto the mountainous cliff.
The king of terror became sad when he swam onto
the shingle. Whale's bone.'

The archer depicted on the lid of the casket (fig. 18) (and labelled *ægili*) may be Weland's brother Egil again, although the scene – in which he defends a building and the (female?) figure inside it against a group of attackers – does not correspond to any story known about him.

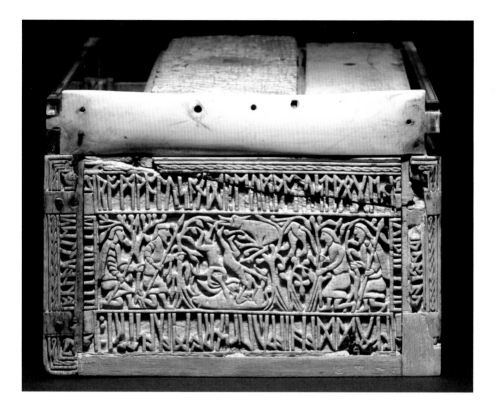

Fig. 19 The left panel
of the casket.

The border inscriptions on the left side and the back of the casket, unlike the one on the front, refer directly to the scenes depicted on the panels. The left side (fig. 19) shows Romulus and Remus being suckled by a wolf. The inscription tells their story briefly (again starting at the top left):

romwalusandreumwalustwœgen | gibroþær | afœddæ hiæwylifinromæcæstri: | oþlæunneg

Rōmwalus and Reumwalus, twǣgen gibrōþær. Afǣdde hiæ wylif in Rōmæcæstri, ōþlæ unnēg.

'Romulus and Remus, two brothers. A she-wolf fed them in Rome, far from their homeland.'

Fig. 20 and *overleaf*
The back of the
casket.

The appearance of this scene on the Undley bracteate (fig. 5) suggests that some version of the story was known in Anglo-Saxon (and/or Continental Germanic) culture even before the arrival of Christianity, but in a Christian context it has added significance. In the Catholic Church of the early Middle Ages, Rome's rise to power was thought to be divinely ordained as a means of spreading the Christian message.

On the back of the casket (fig. 20) is another important event in Christian history – the sacking of Jerusalem and the destruction of its temple by the Roman Emperor Titus in AD 70. The inscription is written in a mixture of (imperfect) Latin and Old English, and uses Roman as well as runic script:

Fig. 21 The cast of the right panel, which has been fitted to the Franks Casket in the collection of the British Museum. The original panel was separated from the casket long ago and is now in the collection of the Museo Nazionale del Bargello in Florence, Italy.

herfegtaþ | + titusendgiuþeasu |
HICFUGIANTHIERUSALIM | **afitatores**

Hēr fegtaþ Titus end giuþeasu. Hīc fugiant Hierusalim afitatores.

'Here Titus and the Jews fight. Here the inhabitants flee Jerusalem.'

The bottom corners contain two shorter sequences of runes: **dom** (Old English *dōm* 'judgement') and **gisl** (*gīsel* 'hostage'). These might serve as captions to the images, or they may represent a name *Dōmgīsl*, perhaps the name of the carver.

The right panel (fig. 21) presents the greatest difficulties to interpretation. The images are assumed to represent

scenes from a heroic legend, possibly the story of Sigurd (which, like the Weland story, we know from medieval Scandinavian sources). In the Icelandic *Völsunga saga*, Sigurd kills Fáfnir, a man who has transformed himself into a dragon. It has been suggested that the figure on the left of the panel is Fáfnir and the armed man opposite him is Sigurd. The three figures on the right have been variously identified as the Norns (supernatural beings who weave the fates of men) or as other human characters from the saga. The inscription is of little help because it is itself very difficult to interpret. It is written in a cipher, the vowel runes being replaced by a set of cryptic characters. The cipher is not terribly complicated, but even once we have solved it, it is not clear what the text is supposed to say. Many interpretations have been proposed, but none of them is entirely convincing.

The interpretations presented here are based on those of respected specialists, but they reflect only a small portion of the literature on the Franks Casket. This fascinating object raises many questions, many of which have not been touched on here: are the panels to be seen as separate scenes and texts covering a variety of themes, or as parts of an overall 'message'? Are they to be viewed and read in a particular order? Why is the inscription on the right side encrypted? After more than a century of scholarly study, the Franks Casket remains both a treasure and a puzzle for scholars.

The end of runic writing in England

The eighth and ninth centuries seem to have been the most productive period of runic inscriptions in England. Probably the latest known English inscription is on a memorial stone at Whithorn in Wigtownshire, Dumfries and Galloway, Scotland (which in the Anglo-Saxon period was part of the kingdom of Northumbria). This stone has been tentatively dated to the late tenth or early eleventh century, and contains part of a personal name. It is perhaps significant that the practice of runic writing survived in the north of Northumbria – the part of Anglo-Saxon England which was most remote from the dominant influence of Wessex, and that had in earlier times produced many of the finest Anglo-Saxon runic monuments, such as the crosses at Bewcastle and Ruthwell (see p. 41). In the south-western kingdom of Wessex – which was the centre of literary culture in England from the late ninth century onwards – it is doubtful whether runes were ever used extensively.

Over the course of the tenth century, as runic writing began to be used less for carving, some scribes maintained an interest in the runes and continued to use them in manuscripts. Manuscript runes seem, for the most part, to belong to the realm of antiquarian scholarship: lists of runes and their names (see chapter 4) often appear alongside texts on cryptography (the art or practice of writing and solving codes), together with other 'exotic' alphabets (both genuine and invented). Some scribes used runes as a sort of secret code in riddles or puzzles, to conceal the solution from the untutored reader. One of the most famous examples is the signature of the poet Cynewulf, spelled out in runes embedded into the text of several poems ascribed to him.

But even as the Anglo-Saxon traditions of runic writing were on the decline, another tradition was being imported by Scandinavian settlers (although apparently not on a large scale). This Scandinavian tradition – the runic writing of the Vikings – is the subject of the next chapter.

CHAPTER THREE

Runes and the Vikings

The extensive journeys of trade, military adventure and exploration in the Viking period (*c*.AD 750–1050) carried Scandinavian people (and their writing) all over Europe. The popular view of Vikings as little more than bloodthirsty, savage pirates has been transformed in recent decades: there is no denying that piracy and warfare were features of the period, but they are far from being the whole story. We are accustomed to tales of savage Viking raiders largely because that is how Scandinavians were perceived and portrayed in the historical records written by their enemies in England and on the Continent. Fortunately, the Viking period – particularly in the later part – is also a period of prolific runic writing. Where the Older Futhark inscriptions and most of the Anglo-Saxon ones are short and often obscure in meaning, in the Viking and later medieval periods (up until *c*.1500) Scandinavian people used runes to write longer texts with more intelligible content. The most prominent examples are the many runestones with memorial inscriptions on them, sometimes with accounts of the lives and deeds of the deceased person.

In the last chapter we looked at how users of runes in England and Frisia adapted the futhark by adding extra characters. In Scandinavia, too, the runic writing system was reorganized during the seventh and eighth centuries, but in quite different ways – the forms of the characters were simplified, and the number of runes was reduced from twenty-four to sixteen.

The sixteen-letter futharks, commonly labelled the 'Younger Futharks', are divided into two main types: the so-called 'long-branch' and 'short-twig' forms. The long-branch runes are commonly associated with Denmark, and the short-twig ones with Sweden and Norway. For this reason the two types are sometimes referred to as 'Danish' and 'Norwegian', (or 'Swedish-Norwegian'), although the distinction is not altogether reliable.

Some of the Younger Futhark runes (particularly **o** and short-twig **b**) have many variant forms. Standardized versions of the long-branch and short-twig futharks are on p. 58.

The long-branch versus short-twig distinction is rather artificial: many inscriptions use runes of both types alongside one another. Fig. 22 shows an example of a futhark using a mixture of forms, carved on a brooch found in England near Penrith, Cumbria:

ᚠᚢᚦᚨ ᚱᚴᚼ ᚻᛁᛆ ᛁᛆᛆ ᛘᛘ

f u þ o r k h n i a s t b m m

The forms of **f u þ o r k** and **i** are common to both types. For most of the other runes, short-twig forms are used (**h n a s t b**), but we have long-branch **m** (the second **m** is perhaps an error for long-branch ᛘ **R**). Short-twig ᚼ **h** is unusual in the British Isles, except on the Isle of Man.

The smaller number of runes and their simpler forms made writing more economical, but as such they can cause difficulties for the reader, as many runes in their new forms

Rune Long-branch	Rune Short-twig	Transliteration	Comments
	ᚠ	f	
	ᚢ	u	
	ᚦ	þ	
	ᚭ	ą o	At an early stage, this rune represented a nasalized [ã]. Later on, this changed to an [o] sound. There are many variant forms besides those given here.
	ᚱ	r	
	ᚴ	k	
ᚼ	ᚼ	h	
ᚾ	ᚾ	n	
	ᛁ	i	
ᛆ	ᛆ	a / æ	
ᛋ	ᛌ	s	
ᛏ	ᛐ	t	
ᛒ	ᛓ	b	
ᛘ / ᛙ	ᛙ	m	
	ᛚ	l	
ᛦ	ᛁ	ʀ / y	Early on, this rune represented a sound somewhere between [z] and [r] (which we conventionally transliterate with ʀ); later, it was used for [y].

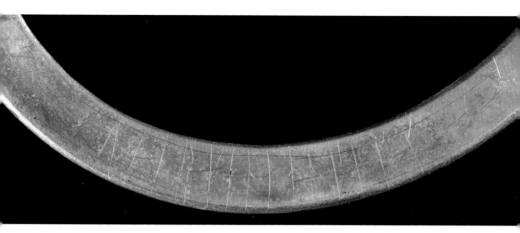

Fig. 22 Detail from the hoop of a silver brooch. Shown here is the runic inscription on the reverse. Viking period, late 9th or early 10th century. Diam. of hoop. 10.4 cm. British Museum 1991,0109.2.

now had to represent several different sounds. For instance, the runes **b t k** each represent two consonants (**b** = [b] and [p], **t** = [t] and [d], **k** = [k] and [g]); while **i** represents both [i] and [e] (long and short). This could make interpretation difficult: the sequence **trik**, for example, can be read as *trik*, *trig*, *dreg*, and so on. To compensate for these problems, several 'dotted' runes were introduced sometime in the tenth or eleventh century to indicate a sound value related to, yet different from, that of the undotted rune. A dotted k, ᛈ for [g] is common, and we sometimes find ᛒ for [p], ᛏ for [d] and ᛐ for [e]. In practice, though, different carvers used them in different ways (and not always consistently). Later on, some carvers added extra runes such as ᛉ for **p**.

Inscriptions using the Younger Futharks

Inscriptions using a sixteen-letter futhark, with or without the later modifications, survive in great numbers in Scandinavia; and they also appear in places to which Scandinavians travelled. We find runes from the Viking period or the later Middle Ages in many parts of the British Isles, the Faroe Islands (situated halfway between Norway and Iceland, between the Norwegian Sea and the North

Atlantic Ocean), Iceland and Greenland; and places as far east as Russia, Ukraine and Turkey.

Runes were carved on a wide variety of portable objects, often with very commonplace, simple contents. A good example of such is the bone comb-case found at Lincoln, England and made in the tenth century (fig. 23). In long-branch runes, the inscription reads:

kamb:koþan:kiari:þorfastr, *Kamb góðan gjarði Þorfastr* 'Þorfastr made a good comb'.

Labelling an object with the name of the maker is a practice we have seen in earlier periods (chapters 1–2), and in this case it seems the maker is actively advertising his wares.

In the later part of the Viking period, runestones commemorating the dead became much more widespread, with particularly large numbers (about 3000) in Sweden. These memorial stones may have had a legal function, as a public declaration of death and an assertion of the right to inherit, though not everyone accepts this interpretation. Their purpose may have been simply one of public commemoration, and/or a display of wealth and power by important local families – having craftsmen carve and raise a runestone, even a relatively simple one, was an

Fig. 23 Bone comb-case. Viking period, 10th century. L.13 cm. British Museum 1867,0320.12.

expensive enterprise. These functions are not mutually exclusive, of course.

Runestone inscriptions are typically formulaic, usually based around the structure 'NN raised this stone after MM, his/her (father/mother/son/daughter…)'. They often include more information – sometimes quite a substantial amount – about the deceased. Many record the person's travels, whether on military adventures, trade, pilgrimage or exploration. Some, for instance, record the deaths of men who took part in Cnut's invasion of England in 1015. At the Hagia Sophia mosque (formerly a Christian cathedral) in Istanbul are runic graffiti which may have been made by mercenaries in the service of the Byzantine Emperor. A group of runestones in Sweden record the deaths of men who participated in an expedition to *Særkland*, which might mean 'the land of the Saracens', i.e., somewhere in the Middle East. Some of the texts are in verse, and contain early evidence for the elaborate metre and inventive metaphors of Viking poetry known as 'skaldic' poetry (from the Old Norse *skald*, meaning 'poet'); but the majority are simpler.

As well as inscriptions, some runestones bear elaborate decorative carvings. One of the most visually impressive runic memorials is from the royal complex at

Jelling in Jutland, Denmark. The Jelling complex includes two
runestones: the smaller is a relatively simple memorial erected
by Gorm, king of Denmark from *c*.936–58, for his wife Þorvi.
Gorm's son, Harald 'Blacktooth' (or 'Bluetooth'), who
reigned from *c*.958–85, set up the larger stone (fig. 24). It is
decorated with intricate interlaced designs, and one face is
covered with an image of the Crucifixion. The inscription,
spread across three surfaces, contains a dedication to both
of Harald's parents and a declaration of his status as a
champion of the Christian faith – making the complex a
display not only of political might but of religious allegiance:

A: **haraltr:kunukʀ:baþ:kaurua**
    kubl:þausi:aft:kurmfaþursin
    aukaft:þãurui:muþur:sina:sa
    haraltr(:)ias:sãʀ:uan:tanmaurk
B: **ala:auknuruiak**
C: **aukt(a)ni(karþi)kristnã**

Haraldr kunungʀ bað gørva kumbl þøsi aft Gorm,
faður sin, ok aft Þõrvi, møður sina. Sa Haraldr æs sæʀ
vann Danmǫrk alla ok Norvæg ok dani gærði kristnã.

'King Haraldr ordered [people] to make these
monuments after Gormr, his father, and after Þorvi, his
mother. That Haraldr who won for himself all Denmark,
and Norway, and made the Danes Christian.' (Text and
translation from Barnes 2012: 73).

The divided futhark and runic ciphers

A very different type of inscription can be seen in the 'Ring
of Brodgar', a large circle of standing stones at Stenness,
Orkney (fig. 25). The site is Neolithic (i.e. it dates to the 'New
Stone Age', *c*.4000–2500 BC), but at some point somebody
carved a cross and series of tree-like signs on one of the slabs.

Fig. 24 The larger
runestone at Jelling in
Jutland, Denmark.

Signs like these 'twig-runes' are well known from the
Viking world; they are one variant of a cipher that depends
on the division of the futhark into three groups of letters
(a group of six and two groups of five):

fuþork / hnias / tbmlʀ.

In the 'twig-rune' cipher, the number of twigs on one side
of the vertical indicates the group, and the number of twigs

Fig. 25 Plaster cast of the twig-runes and cross on one of the stones in the Neolithic Ring of Brodgar, in Orkney. L. 23.5 cm. British Museum 1908,0221.1.

on the other side indicates the rune within that group. Normally (but not always), the order of the groups is reversed, so that a twig-rune 1/4 stands for the fourth rune of the third (not the first) group, **l** (see fig. 26).

In the Brodgar inscription, the second character from the left is not a twig-rune; it is usually read as r in a rather open and misshapen form. If we accept this and read the rest of the inscription (from right to left) using the '6-5-5' cipher outlined above, it gives us the apparently meaningless sequence **niorn** or **nuorn** (one of the runes is damaged, and could be either 3/2 **u** or 2/2 **i**). One runologist, Magnus Olsen, read the inscription as **biorn** (treating the rightmost twig-rune as 1/2), representing the man's name *Bjǫrn*; but this reading is disputed. There are also questions

	Rune 1	2	3	4	5	6
Group 1	f	u	þ	o	r	k
Group 2	h	n	i	a	s	
Group 3	t	b	m	l	R/y	

Fig. 26 The '6-5-5' cipher.

about the authenticity of the inscription. Several of the stones in the ring bear graffiti, some dated to the nineteenth century, and it is possible that the twig-runes (whatever their intended meaning) are also modern.

The 6-5-5 cipher appears in many different inscriptions and in a number of different forms, such as fish with different numbers of spines either side of their bodies. Several ciphers of this sort are displayed on the ninth-century Rök stone in Östergötland, Sweden, and 'twig-runes' (in two variants) are also found in graffiti at Maeshowe[4] in Orkney, shown below:

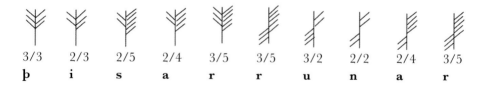

| 3/3 | 2/3 | 2/5 | 2/4 | 3/5 | 3/5 | 3/2 | 2/2 | 2/4 | 3/5 |
| þ | i | s | a | r | r | u | n | a | r |

þessar rúnar 'These runes' (after Barnes 2012: 150–51). This is an abbreviation of the common formula 'I [name] carved these runes'.

These ciphers may have been used for many different purposes, one being as a demonstration of skill in the use and understanding of the script, to present a 'secret message' which could only be read by those with the necessary learning. The challenge of solving the puzzle may be more important than the content of the hidden message. This Maeshowe example illustrates the point: twig-runes are used here to 'conceal' a message which is in no way secret.

The later Middle Ages and beyond

Following a fire in 1955, archaeological excavations in the Bryggen district of Bergen – a major medieval trading centre in Norway – revealed hundreds of *rúnakefli*, that is wooden sticks carved with runic messages. Smaller collections of *rúnakefli* have been found in other medieval Scandinavian towns, and the amount and variety of material seems to indicate widespread runic literacy in this period. What makes them so interesting and useful for modern study is that they give us a sample of Norse language as used by ordinary people in the later Middle Ages (most of the inscriptions date from the thirteenth and fourteenth centuries), and reveal the wide range of purposes for which they used runic writing: they include personal messages, business letters, jokes, prayers and apparently meaningless strings of runes. A database of the Bergen sticks is available online (see Further reading, p. 104). One of these inscriptions is shown here (fig. 27; B055 in the online database).

The text reads **her:færr:hafdiæfr** 'Hafdjarfr sails here', and is appropriately accompanied by the image of three ships. The name Hafdjarfr may be a nickname: it literally

Fig. 27 Detail of one of the many *rúnakefli* – wooden sticks with runic inscriptions – recovered in Bergen, Norway. c.13th or 14th century. Maritime Museum, Bergen, Norway.

means something like 'sea-daring', which is very apt for the text and the images. The runes transliterated **e** and **d** are dotted **i** and **t**, respectively. This may simply have been carved for amusement.

Here are a few more inscriptions from Bergen (you can find pictures in the online database):

B085

auimaria
[Latin]: *Ave Maria*.

This and other Latin prayers are quite common in the Bergen material. They do not necessarily mean that the carvers were competent in Latin; formulaic prayers would likely have been familiar to everyone.

B100

[..](ø)rgniæs:dpy:fu:fo:fi:fy:uf:uþ:u[...]
(Transliteration from Seim 1991:124).

The first part of this apparently meaningless sequence is probably a rather scrambled futhark (**g** and **d** are dotted runes; **p** is the character Κ; see p. 59). The remainder is a string of syllables beginning with each rune of the futhark in sequence (first **f** with four of the five vowel-runes; then **u** with the consonants in order). Several inscriptions from Bergen and elsewhere contain similar sequences and were likely intended for practice in writing, giving us an insight into how knowledge of the runic script was taught and learned. A magical interpretation (with the nonsense syllables as part of an incantation, reminiscent of the **ærkriu...** sequence on the 'amulet rings'; pp. 84–5) is conceivable, but less likely. As our other examples show, the rune-carvers in Bergen more often had their minds on worldly matters.

B0139

æirikra
Eirikr á
'Eirikr owns'

Many of the inscriptions from Bergen are very short,
consisting of personal names, often with the verb *á* 'owns'.
Some of these are on wooden tags used to mark goods
that a person had bought.

B0149

kya:sæhir:atþu:kakhæim
þãnsak:aƀakistãn:rþis
Gyða segir at þú gakk heim. [?].
'Gyða says you (are to) go home.'

While some of the texts express pious sentiments and
some seem to be charms, this and others have more earthy,
everyday subjects. The second line of text (**þãnsak…**)
may have been an attempt at a reply to the stern message
relayed from Gyða (whoever she might have been), but it
is incomprehensible. Perhaps the respondent was not very
literate (considering that this stick was found in a tavern),
or perhaps he or she had fulfilled the wish expressed in
the next example.

B308

mynta:ek:myklu oꝑdaꝛ miǫþ:ranci koma nãla
Mynda ek miklu optar mjǫðranns til koma nála
'I would much rather visit the mead-house more often!'
(Text and translation from Spurkland 2005: 190).

We do not know why this carver felt the need to record his or her fondness for the mead-house, nor do we know to whom the message was directed; but the casual nature of the text illustrates the point that – in late medieval Bergen, at least – writing in runes should not be seen as a rarefied activity reserved for special purposes, but as a form of everyday communication.

By *c.*1500, runic writing had died out in most parts of Scandinavia, but it survived in some areas perhaps as recently as the eighteenth or even the nineteenth century. It is often difficult to tell whether these apparent survivals represent an ongoing tradition or a revived one inspired by antiquarian interests. Sticks carved with runic 'calendars' seem to have been quite popular: the earliest known examples are from the thirteenth century, and many examples survive from the post-Reformation period. Fig. 28 is an example of this kind of calendar. The image shows a repeated sequence of seven runes representing the days of the week. Another row of runes and/or other symbols represents the nineteen years of the lunar cycle, which is important for calculating the date of Easter.

More recently, various people around the world have revived the use of runes, sometimes for amusement or the creation of artworks (such as the finger-ring shown *overleaf*, fig. 29), and sometimes in the creation of forgeries. The most notorious and clear-cut case of runic forgery was a piece of bone carved with Older Futhark runes, 'discovered' during an archaeological dig on the Maria Saaler Berg in Austria in 1924. Eventually one of the workers at the site confessed to having made the carvings himself, but not before it had been published and widely discussed by runologists. There are many other inscriptions known to be, or suspected of being, modern creations, but

Fig. 28 Runic calendar made from wood and shaped like a sword. Norway, date unknown. L. 117.5 cm. British Museum 1858,0705.1. Donated by Henry Woodfall Crowe.

Fig. 29 Gilded bronze finger-ring. 19th century (?). This is a replica or imitation of the Kingmoor ring, with an inscription thought to contain a magic charm (see p. 85). Diam. 2.8 cm. British Museum 1959,0209.27. Bequeathed by Miss Marie Francis Talbot Ready.

the intentions of the people who made them are often unclear. The runestone at Kensington, Minnesota in mid-western USA is one such case. It was discovered in 1898 and has excited fierce controversy ever since. Most runologists believe it to be modern, but it is not clear whether it was made with the intent to deceive (a deliberate forgery) or for some other purpose. Likewise, if the Brodgar twig-runes (pp. 62–3) are modern, we do not know who made them or why.

CHAPTER FOUR

The rune-names

One of the most widely known properties of runic writing is that each rune has a name, a meaningful word beginning (in most cases) with the sound that the character represents – so the name for **f**, for example, is Old English *feoh*, Old Norse *fé*, both meaning 'cattle' or 'wealth'. The exceptions to the principle of naming by the initial sound (the 'acrophonic principle') are **ŋ** and **z**, because they represent sounds which cannot be word-initial in any Germanic language. The name recorded for **ŋ** is *Ing*, believed to be the name of a legendary hero. The case of **z** is a little more complicated: the extant lists of rune-names were compiled at a time when the sound [z] had been lost. In Old English sources, the rune Ⴟ has been used for a different sound, although it is often assumed that its name *eolhx(secg)* is derived from a word meaning 'elk' or 'protection'.

Lists of runes and rune-names – either in futhark order or arranged like the Roman alphabet – appear in a number of medieval manuscripts, often alongside various other alphabets. Some of these lists are based on the Anglo-Saxon futhorc, others on the Scandinavian Younger Futharks. None of the manuscript lists is older than the ninth century, and most seem to be the work of scribes unfamiliar with runic writing. The manuscript traditions reflect, for the most part, a scholarly interest in archaic, exotic and/or cryptic writing systems.

Perhaps the most useful of the manuscript sources are the three 'rune poems'– verse texts which contain a stanza explaining the name of each rune. The earliest of the rune poems was written in Old English and preserved in a late tenth or eleventh-century manuscript, but it survives only in a copy made for the scholar George Hickes in the eighteenth century. It contains twenty-nine stanzas, each beginning with the rune, its Roman-alphabet equivalent and the rune-name. Here is the first stanza:

ᚠ F *feoh býþ frofur. fira gehwýlcum. sceal ðeah manna gehwýlc. miclun hýt dælan. gif he wile. for drihtne domes hleotan*

'*Feoh* [wealth] is a comfort to everyone; but each person must give it away freely, if he wants to receive glory in the sight of the Lord.' (Text, including punctuation, from Hickes's copy (fig. 30). Author's translation).

The other rune poems are from Iceland and Norway, and contain sixteen stanzas each (for the runes of the Younger Futhark). They are much later in date: the oldest surviving text of the Icelandic poem is from the fifteenth century, while the Norwegian poem is not recorded until the seventeenth, although both are based on older sources. The first stanza of the Icelandic poem reads:

ᚠ *er frænda rog ok flædar viti ok grafseiðs gata.*

'ᚠ is family strife and men's delight and grave-fish's path.' (Text and translation from Page 1998).

The Norwegian text (in the version most often cited today, derived from a late nineteenth-century edition) is:

ᚠ *(fé) vældr frénda róge; fødesk ulfr í skóge.*

'ᚠ (wealth) causes trouble among relatives; the wolf lives

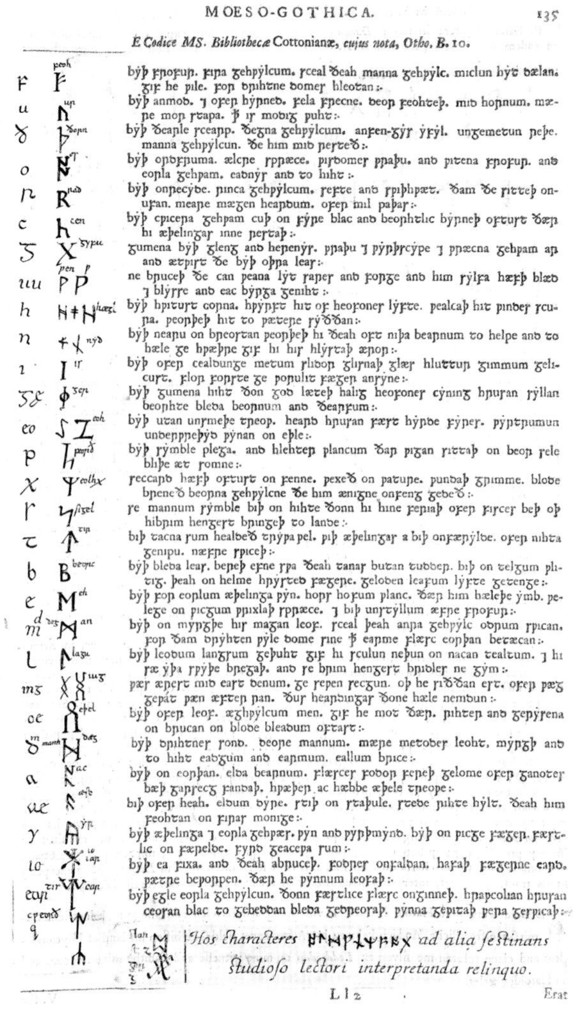

Fig. 30 Page from
George Hicke's
manuscript. This
18th-century copy
of an earlier late
10th-/11th-century
manuscript preserves
the earliest of the
rune-poems, from
which we can learn
about the tradition
of rune-names.

in the forest.' (Text and translation from Halsall 1981).

It should be emphasized that the versions of the Icelandic
and Norwegian poems here are the result of heavy editing;
in the manuscripts and early editions there is considerable
variation of spelling, and to a lesser extent content.

The Norwegian and Icelandic texts are very different from the Old English one in both structure and meaning, but all three agree on the name 'wealth'. There is also agreement on many of the other names (for example, **m** is Old English *mann*, Old Norse *maðr* meaning 'man,' or 'person'). For others, the form of the name is similar but the meaning is not: the name of **u** is *ūr* in all three poems, but the meanings indicated are 'aurochs' for the Old English, 'drizzle' for the Icelandic, and 'slag' for the Norwegian. For some runes, entirely different names appear: the names for **þ** are Old English *þorn* 'thorn', Old Norse *þurs* 'giant,' or 'demon'. We do not know whether one of these was the 'original' name of the rune and the other replaced it, or whether they represent two separate traditions.

Here is a rather simplified list of Old English and Old Norse rune-names and their meanings (some of which are less clear than others). A more detailed account can be found in Page (1999), chapter 5:

Old English	Old Norse
ᚠ *feoh* 'wealth'	ᚠ *fě* 'wealth'
ᚢ *ūr* 'aurochs(?)'	ᚢ *úr* 'drizzle' (Icelandic)
	úr 'slag' (Norwegian)
ᚦ *þorn* 'thorn'	ᚦ *þurs* 'giant; demon'
ᚩ *ōs* 'mouth'	ᚬ *óss* 'god' (Icelandic)
	óss 'river-mouth' (Norwegian)
ᚱ *rād* 'journey, riding'	ᚱ *reið* 'riding' (Icelandic)
	ræið 'riding' (Norwegian)
ᚳ *cēn* 'torch'	ᚴ *kaun* 'sore, ulcer'
ᚷ *gyfu* 'gift'	
ᚹ *wynn* 'joy'	

Old English	Old Norse
ᚻ *hægl* 'hail'	ᚼ *hagal(l)* 'hail'
ᚾ *nȳd* 'need, affliction'	ᚾ nauðr 'constraint' (this is a cognate of nȳd)
ᛁ *īs* 'ice'	ᛁ *ís* 'ice'
ᛄ *gēr* '(good, fruitful) year'	ᛅ *ár* '(good, fruitful) year'
ᛇ ēoh 'yew'	
ᛈ *peorð* (meaning unknown. Various suggestions have been made, but none is convincing).	
ᛉ *eolhx(secg)* 'a kind of sedge-grass'.	
ᛋ *sigel* 'sun'	ᛋ *sól* 'sun'
ᛏ *tir* 'a guiding star or constellation'	ᛏ *Týr* 'the god Týr'
ᛒ *beorc* 'birch'	ᛒ *bjarkan* 'birch-twig'
ᛖ *eh* 'horse'	
ᛗ man 'man, person'	ᛘ maðr 'man, person'
ᛚ *lagu* 'water'	ᛚ *lǫgr* 'water'
	ᛦ ýr 'yew' (compare the Old English name for ᛖ).
ᛝ ing 'the hero Ing'	
ᛟ eþel 'land, ancestral home'	
ᛞ dæg 'day'	
ᚪ ac 'oak'	
ᚫ æsc 'ash-tree'	
ᚣ yr (meaning uncertain; possibly 'bow', 'horn' or 'saddle')	
ᛡ iar (other manuscripts have ior) 'fish? eel? boat?'	
ᛠ ear 'earth? grave?'	

The additional Northumbrian runes (see p. 36) do not appear in the Old English rune poem, but other manuscript sources record names for two of them:

ᛣ **k** = *calc*, which might mean 'chalk' or 'cup' or 'sandal';
ᚸ **ḡ** = *gār* 'spear'.

It is common in both scholarly and popular accounts of the rune-names to find a list of reconstructed names in an early form of Germanic language, with the implication that these represent the 'original' rune-names (e.g., ᚠ = **fehu* 'wealth'; ᚨ = **ansuz* 'god'; the names are marked with an asterisk to show that they are reconstructions, not attested forms). The lists of names in the manuscript sources agree with one another to a large degree, and this suggests that they genuinely reflect an earlier tradition of rune-names. We cannot be sure, however, that this tradition was the 'original' one (that is, a tradition of rune-names used in the period of the earliest inscriptions), or that there was only one 'original' set of rune-names.

Two types of evidence may support the idea that the known rune-names, or perhaps some others, existed in early epigraphical tradition. Firstly, changes in the sound-values of runes appear to be reflected in some of their names. For instance, the reconstructed early form of the word 'year' is **jara-* or **jēra-*, which gives us Old English *gear* (the *g-* here is pronounced like [j]). In Old Norse, the initial [j] is lost, but the name *ár* 'year' is retained and applied to the new **a**-rune. We might, then, reasonably argue that the name 'year' for the **j**-rune existed before this sound-change took place (possibly around the time when the futhark was reduced to sixteen characters).

The second type of evidence is the use of individual runes as abbreviations for their names. This sort of abbreviation (often known by the German term *Begriffsrune* 'idea-rune') is found in Anglo-Saxon manuscripts: scribes

sometimes used ᛗ for Old English *mann/monn* 'man, person'
and ᛞ for *dæg*, for example. Epigraphical examples are very
scarce: the most frequently cited one is on the seventh-
century stone at Stentoften in Blekinge, Sweden. Part of
the inscription reads **hAþuwolAfzgAfj**, which is usually
interpreted as *Haþuwolfaz gaf j(ara/-ēra)*, 'Haþuwulfaz gave
a good/fruitful year' (A represents an additional rune ᛉ,
used in some late Older Futhark inscriptions). Perhaps the
clearest example of a single rune standing for a word that
we can easily identify is on a bracteate found at Sievern in
northern Germany, with the inscription **rwrilu** (fig. 31).
l is almost certainly an error for **t**, and the whole text is
interpretable as *r[ūnōz] wrītu* 'I write runes' – a common
formula for inscriptions. Here **r** seems to stand for a whole
word, but the word is *rūnōz* 'runes' (or the singular *rūnā*
'rune, inscription'), which is not an attested name for the
r-rune. The Sievern inscription would suggest that in the
rare cases where a single rune is used as an abbreviation,
it does not necessarily stand for the rune-name. The
epigraphical evidence that we have for this kind of
abbreviation suggests that the practice was not very
common, and it is of limited use as evidence for rune-
names in the early period of runic writing.

Another difficulty for the reconstruction of 'original'
rune-names is the fact that we have only sixteen names in
the Scandinavian lists; for the rest, we have to rely on the
Anglo-Saxon sources. It is possible to reconstruct older
forms of the Old English names (e.g., **wunjō* for *wynn* 'joy'),
but we have no way of knowing if the attested Old English
names are inherited from an early tradition, or if they
replaced older ones. In the case of *peorð*, we cannot be
certain what the Old English word means, let alone what
the earlier name or names might have been.

Speculation about the earliest set of rune-names has
led to various theories about their relationship with early

Germanic culture or cosmology. These theories start from the assumption that the names were not just common words that happened to begin (or end, in the case of **ŋ** and **z**) with the appropriate sounds, but represented important ideas in the culture of the people who used them. There are some obvious connections in meaning between names such as 'day', 'year' and 'sun' (all relating to the measurement of time, which is essential in a culture reliant on agriculture); or 'oak', 'ash', 'yew' and 'thorn' (names of trees). The significance of these patterns is, however, uncertain. There is little justification for assuming an overall semantic 'system' behind all the rune-names, especially as we cannot be certain what the 'original' ones were. Even more dubious is the popular belief that the rune-names are a key to the esoteric power of runic symbols (see chapter 6).

Fig. 31 Gold bracteate found at Sievern, Niedersachsen, Germany. 5th century. Diam. 2.5 cm. Historisches Museum Bremerhaven, Germany.

CHAPTER FIVE

The work of runologists

Runology – the academic study of runes and runic inscriptions – is an eclectic field, drawing on a range of disciplines including linguistics, archaeology, art history, literary and cultural history. Specialists in each of these areas bring to bear their own particular interests, methods and theoretical backgrounds in the effort to understand both the inscriptions and the cultural contexts in which they were created. Partly because of this diversity of approaches, scholars sometimes come to very different conclusions about the interpretation and cultural significance of a particular inscription. As we have seen in earlier chapters, considerable uncertainty surrounds the reading and interpretation of even quite simple inscriptions.

Part of the reason for this uncertainty is the nature of the evidence, especially in the early period. The Older Futhark was in use for at least 500 years, yet we know of only about 400 objects with Older Futhark inscriptions. An observation famous among runologists is that if there were only ten people living at any one time who were capable of writing with runes, and each of them produced only ten inscriptions per year, there would be 40,000 inscriptions made between AD 200 and 600, of which we have less than 1%. The precise figures are not important, but the point is well made that even if runic writing was a very rare and specialized skill in this period, to which only a few were privy (and we have very little evidence for or against this possibility), the corpus of inscriptions so far discovered must be only a small proportion of those that were actually made. For later periods in certain places (the most striking example being medieval Bergen), the quantity of material is much larger, but we still do not know how representative it is.

Object and context

As we noted at the very beginning, in order to understand the content of an inscription, an understanding of linguistic details is absolutely essential; but the starting point for the runologist is the careful examination of the inscribed object and its context, and so the skills of the archaeologist and the art historian come into play before those of the linguist. By gathering as much information as we possibly can about the object – its material, the techniques used for carving runes, any accompanying decoration and and its archaeological context – we can begin to piece together the stories behind the inscription: what has been written, by whom and why.

We do not always have access to this sort of information, however. Archaeological methods in the nineteenth century were not so rigorous as they are today, and so for objects uncovered in older excavations we do not have as much detail about the context in which they were found. Some objects – such as the Undley bracteate (pp. 26–7) – are loose finds, found on the surface of the ground (for example, after ploughing or construction work), or discovered with metal detectors. Other objects only come to the attention of scholars after they have been in private hands for some time, and we simply do not know how they were acquired or what their earlier history might have been. One example is the 'Bateman' brooch (pp. 22–3), which came to the British Museum from a private collection, with no information about its earlier history except that it was reported to have been found somewhere in Kent.

If we do not have an archaeological context, we can still glean some useful information from the object itself. The material of an object and the way it has been made or decorated can help us identify approximately when and where an object was made, and hint at to whom it might have belonged, and all such information can help us as we try to interpret the inscription.

Difficulties of reading and interpretation

Fig. 32 Iron spearhead with inlaid motifs inscribed at the base of the blade. Found in Buckland in Dover, England. Anglo-Saxon. Late 5th–early 7th century. British Museum 1995,0102.392. Donated by Orbit Housing Association.

As well as general questions about the cultural context of runic writing, we are faced with more specific difficulties in extracting meaning from individual inscriptions. As has already been made clear, deciphering runes can sometimes be difficult, if they have become illlegible through time, and deliberate carvings may be difficult to distinguish from unintentional scratches. Perhaps the characters are hard to identify or recognize because the carver was unfamiliar with the script, or was unskilled with his or her tools, or used unusual letter-forms: the Loveden Hill inscription

(pp. 84–87) begins with recognizable runic characters, but they become less and less identifiable as we read from left to right, until we can no longer be sure whether what we are looking at is still writing or just a string of signs that are purely symbolic or perhaps meaningless. Sometimes markings on objects look 'rune-like' or 'runic' , but they do not represent writing. One example is a spearhead from a cemetery at Buckland, Dover (fig. 32). The spearhead has two inlaid motifs which have sometimes been called 'runic', although they are certainly not runes.

The arrow shape resembles a **t**-rune, but it forms part of what clearly seems to be a stylized bow and arrow. Other spearheads are known from Germany and eastern Europe with similar abstract symbols, sometimes alongside 'genuine' runes. These motifs surely meant something to the people who made them, but we can do little more than speculate about what that might have been.

Even if we can identify the runes, it is not always possible to make sense of them: some inscriptions consist partly or wholly of strings of characters that are legible but cannot be rendered into comprehensible language, such as the 'Bateman' brooch. These sequences might be entirely meaningless, produced by an illiterate carver for an illiterate audience in imitation of 'real' writing. For example, some bracteates have meaningful runic inscriptions (like Undley, even if its inscription is difficult to interpret), but others are inscribed with apparently nonsensical sequences of runes and/or Roman letters, or letter-like shapes.

Magical interpretations have been proposed for some of these sequences, but most are speculative at best. An outstanding exception – where we have good reason to believe that an apparently nonsensical inscription had a magical function, and we have some evidence for what that function was – can be found in the inscription on an Anglo-Saxon finger-ring reportedly found in Kingmoor in Cumbria, England (fig. 33). The inscription reads:

ærkriufltkriuriþonglæstæpontol.

This cannot be rendered into meaningful Old English (or any other language, although parts of it resemble Irish words). Similar sequences appear on two other Anglo-Saxon rings, and on a stick from Bergen (B607 in the online database – see p. 66). A clue to their possible purpose comes from two versions of an Old English charm for staunching blood, recorded in a tenth-century manuscript. The charm requires the user to recite a string of nonsense words, including *ærcrio* or *ærcræ*. We cannot be certain, but the similarity to the charm-text suggests that these inscriptions might have been intended to protect the wearer against bleeding wounds.

It is thanks to the widespread practice (particularly among pre-Christian peoples) of burying the dead with grave-goods that many of the surviving objects with runic inscriptions have been discovered. Two early Anglo-Saxon grave-finds can help to illustrate the importance of studying an inscription as a cultural artefact and not just as a piece of text: the Loveden Hill urn and Chessell Down Pail.

The Loveden Hill urn
This cremation urn (fig. 34), probably made in the sixth century, is one of hundreds excavated from a cemetery at Loveden Hill in Lincolnshire, England. The practice of cremating the dead and burying their remains in pottery

Fig. 33 Gold finger-ring engraved with runic inscription. Found in Kingmoor in Cumbria, England. Anglo-Saxon, 8th–10th century. Diam. 2.7 cm. British Museum OA.10262. Donated by George Hamilton Gordon, 4th Earl of Aberdeen.

urns is common in this period, both in eastern parts of Britain and in the Continental regions from which Anglo-Saxon migrants are thought to have come (chiefly northern Germany and Jutland, Denmark – see chapter 3). Like those at other sites, many of the urns from Loveden Hill are decorated with lines, geometric patterns and symbols, some of them 'rune-like'; but this is the only one with a runic 'text' (that is, a series of runes that can be interpreted as a piece of language). It is not made from local clay (unlike most of the urns at Loveden Hill), and so was probably imported from elsewhere. It is not possible to learn much from the fragments of bone found in the urn. The objects found with it, however, indicate that the deceased was probably a woman.

As was mentioned earlier, the inscription itself consists of a legible sequence **siþæbæd**, followed by several more characters which might or might not be additional runes.

It is generally agreed that **sïþæbæd** represents either a (probably) feminine personal name *Sīþabad*, or a masculine one *Sīþabald* (with the *l* missing). If the name is masculine, it is unlikely to belong to the deceased. It might be the signature of the potter who made the urn, but there are no other urns with personal names written on them, so this was clearly not a normal practice for craftspeople.

Several readings and interpretations have been proposed for the characters after **sïþæbæd**, but all are doubtful. One suggestion is that they include the Old English word *hlǽw* 'grave'. If this is correct, it might imply that the name does belong to the woman whose remains are contained in the urn. This interpretation is rather appealing, but it leaves us with difficult (and unanswerable) questions about the history of the object. If the woman was local, and if this was her name, and if the urn was not made locally, does that mean that it was specially commissioned from and inscribed by a craftsman in another community? If so, why? The same sequence has also been interpreted as *hlāf* 'bread', which perhaps signifys prosperity (this appears to be the idea underlying the Old English words *hlaford* 'lord' and *hlæfdige* 'lady', which literally mean something like 'bread-guardian' and 'bread-kneader'). Again, this is a very speculative treatment of characters that might not be meaningful letters at all, but an imitation of writing by a partially illiterate individual.

Fig. 34 The Loveden Hill urn. Handmade pottery recovered from a cemetery in Lincolnshire, England. Early Anglo-Saxon, probably 6th century. H. 25.3 cm. British Museum 1963,1001.14.

The Chessell Down pail

The cemetery at Chessell Down on the Isle of Wight was mentioned in chapter 2, where we looked at the inscription on a scabbard mount. The pail pictured in fig. 35 comes from a woman's grave at the same site. Both of the burials containing inscribed objects were inhumations (that is, the body was buried intact and not cremated), and

both contained a rich array of grave-goods, suggesting
that the people occupying them were relatively wealthy
and important members of the local community.
Furthermore, both of the inscribed objects show that this
was a community which was involved in Continental
trading networks. The scabbard mount belonged to a
sword with a complex history: the pommel (the enlarged

fitting at the top of the handle) is thought to be Scandinavian (or perhaps a Kentish imitation of a Scandinavian style), while the blade was likely made in the Rhineland. The scabbard mount with the runic inscription is a replacement for a lost original; it could have been made and inscribed before the sword was imported to England, but is perhaps more likely to be of local manufacture.

The pail is also an import, made somewhere in the eastern Mediterranean; a similar pail (without an inscription) was found in another grave at Chessell Down. Again, the runes might have been added before the pail found its way to the Isle of Wight, but it was probably done in England and quite possibly locally.

The inscription on the pail is not clearly legible, but can be partially transliterated **...bw(s)...ekkkaaa**. The Dutch runologist Tineke Looijenga has suggested that it might represent a cryptic formula concealing three personal names, *Becca, Wecca, Secca* (Looijenga 2003: 280–1). This suggestion is inspired by a cipher found in several Scandinavian inscriptions: the apparently obscure sequence **þmkiiissstttiiillll** can be resolved into three rhyming words, *þistill, mistill, kistill* meaning 'thistle, mistletoe, little chest'. The significance of this formula is unknown (though there has been speculation that it is connected with burial rites). If Looijenga's interpretation of the Chessell Down inscription is correct, the import of the names *Becca, Wecca, Secca* is equally obscure. Nonetheless, when we look at the two Chessell Down inscriptions together and in their archaeological context, they hint at the possible existence of a local practice of rune-writing, perhaps associated with the wealthier members of the community who added runes to their property for reasons that remain unclear.

As these two examples show, trying to understand a runic inscription is rarely a simple matter. In order to find

Fig. 35 *overleaf* Detail from the brass Chessell Down pail. Found at the cemetery at Chessell Down on the Isle of Wight. It was most probably made somewhere in the eastern Mediterranean in the 6th century. H. 11.5 cm; diam. 17.7 cm. British Museum 1867,0729.136.

meaning in an inscription, we have to study it as part of an object and as a product of a living human society. When we attempt to interpret it, we are attempting to reconstruct the language of the people who made it, as well as the culture in which those people lived and died. Even when we bring together all the available evidence, what we are left with is not 'truth', but a set of enticing clues which can help us to form plausible theories about the linguistic and cultural meanings of an inscription.

CHAPTER SIX

Runes in the modern world

Many people have an interest in history and language. We continue to be fascinated by the period of European history which is still lamentably and inaccurately called the 'Dark Ages' (roughly speaking, from the fifth to the eleventh centuries AD), and especially by the adventurous spirit of the Viking Age. Aside from genuine historical interest, though, runes have entered popular culture and popular consciousness largely due to their supposed magical properties.

Runes appear occasionally in fantasy or mystery literature of the early twentieth century, such as M.R. James's story *Casting the Runes*, in which the antagonist, Karswell, murders his enemies by means of a curse written in runes. However, it is to J.R.R. Tolkien that the genre owes the greatest debt. Like James, Tolkien was a medieval scholar, who was familiar with Old English and Old Norse language, literature and mythology. In *The Hobbit*, the clues which reveal the secret entrance to the Lonely Mountain are written in 'Dwarvish' writing, which Tolkien represented by adapting Anglo-Saxon runes. For *The Lord*

of the Rings he created his own Dwarvish script using runic
and rune-like letters with sound values unrelated to their
historical ones. Since then, many authors, film directors
and game designers have incorporated runes into their
works. Sadly, there is seldom any connection between these
fantasy runes and real ones; they are usually presented not
as a form of writing at all, but merely as a set of magic
symbols, each with its own iconic powers (such as a fire
rune, a chaos rune, and so on).

Runes have also infamously been appropriated for
political purposes. The National Socialist regime in
Germany used runes as symbols of national and racial
identity, inspired by the belief of some mystically-inclined
nationalists that runes were holy symbols, encoding the
power and secret knowledge of the ancient Aryans.
The 'double lightning' emblem of the SS consists of two
ᛋ-runes, supposedly representing not only the organization's
name, *Schutzstaffel* ('Protection Squadron'), but also the
invented rune-name *sig* 'victory'. Other Nazi organizations
used runes in their insignia, with meanings inspired by their
historically attested names, and/or invented ones. Some
of these runic (or perhaps we should say rune-inspired)
symbols have been adopted by neo-Nazi organizations in
Europe and North America. Examples are the 'Life-Rune'
logo of the National Alliance in the United States (a
form of ᛉ), or the ᛏ-rune used by *Svenska Motståndsrörelsen*
('Swedish Resistance Movement').

Perhaps the most prevalent use of runes in the present
day is in the arena of New-Age or pagan magic. A quick
online search will turn up dozens of books and websites
devoted to the use of runes for divination, magic and
self-help. Like the fantasy literature and Nazi iconography
mentioned already, the majority of modern pagan work
uses runes (usually the runes of the Older Futhark) as iconic
symbols with esoteric meanings inspired by their names.
Most pagan books or websites will mention the historical

use of runes as writing, but this is generally treated as something secondary to their symbolic and oracular functions.

It would obviously be unjust to draw direct parallels between fantasy literature, modern paganism and political extremism. In their use of runes, though, these three areas of culture are informed by a shared set of (thoroughly modern) ideas. The most important of these are that runes are inherently magical; that they are first and foremost iconic symbols, only secondarily and incidentally functioning as written letters; and that their power or significance is expressed chiefly through the rune-names. We do not have enough space here to discuss the issue in detail, but some historical background may be helpful.

A crucial factor affecting modern perceptions of the medieval and pre-medieval past is the growth of nationalist thought in the eighteenth and nineteenth centuries. For some Scandinavian, German and English scholars of this period, runic inscriptions offered an insight into their national (and racial) origins. By the end of the nineteenth century, the so-called *völkisch* movement was gaining popularity in Germany and Austria. Its main aim was to encourage a shared sense of German ethnic and national identity by creating and promoting a romantic narrative of the past. Taking inspiration from Tacitus's *Germania*, this narrative was often framed in terms of an opposition between corrupt, over-sophisticated Rome and the virtuous, racially pure barbarians beyond the Rhine frontier. The manifestations of the *völkisch* movement could be as innocuous as hiking and rowing clubs bound together by a love of the national landscape, but some of its adherents also had overtly political motives. The period of *völkisch* nationalism was also one in which new religions were springing up, one of the most prominent being the Theosophy movement founded by the Russian-German Helena Petrovna Blavatsky in 1875. At the core of

Blavatsky's world view was the idea that all the world's religions stem from a single spiritual tradition of great antiquity. Humanity was supposed to be in a process of spiritual evolution through seven 'root-races'; Europeans were said to be descendants of the ancient Aryans, the fifth 'root-race', while 'lesser' races of modern humans were depicted as the degenerate offspring of the earlier root-races, or the result of racial miscegenation (the interbreeding of different races).

Rune-magic, *völkisch* romanticism and Blavatskyan mystical racism came together in the work of the Austrian occultist Guido List. In a series of books published in the early years of the twentieth century, List revealed the secret knowledge of the ancient 'Aryo-Germans', who supposedly represented the purest branch of the Aryan race. The most influential of his works was *Das Geheimnis der Runen*, 'The Secret of the Runes' (1908). List claimed that a section of the medieval Icelandic poem *Hávamál* ('The sayings of the High One') contained the key to the meanings of the Aryo-German 'Futharkh', an eighteen-letter rune-row based on the Younger Futhark. The final rune of List's 'Futharkh', said to represent the greatest mystery of the Aryo-Germans (the union of the human and the divine), was the swastika.

List's influence helped to popularize the idea that runes were ancient holy symbols which encoded esoteric knowledge in their names, their forms and their sounds. He inspired a generation of rune-occultists who combined runes with ideas taken from astrology, Freemasonry and Indian spiritual practices in the 1920s and 1930s. They were not always treated sympathetically by the Nazi authorities: many of them, such as Friedrich Bernhard Marby (who invented a system of 'rune-gymnastics', using body postures that imitated the shapes of runes), were denounced as cranks. Marby suffered particularly harsh treatment, spending several years in a string of

Fig. 36 Silver SS 'Death's head ring', inscribed on the inside 'S. lb. Baltes [To his dear Baltes] 21.6.43 H. Himmler'. Diam. approx. 2.7 cm. Kreismuseum Wewelsburg, Germany, inventory no. 15907.

concentration camps. On the other hand, Karl Maria Wiligut (who seems to have had a hand in Marby's downfall) rose to prominence in the SS and became part of Heinrich Himmler's inner circle. He designed many of the symbols and practices of the SS, including the *Totenkopfring* ('Death's head ring') (fig. 36).

These rings (officially known as *SS-Ehrenringe* 'SS honour rings') were awarded to SS officers in return for their service, and were supposed to remind the wearer of proper 'Germanic' and National Socialist values. On the inside of the ring above is a personal dedication from Himmler, and on the outside five 'runic' symbols: two **s**-runes; **h** in a form based on the long-branch ᚼ; a swastika; and, placed together in a circular field, the so-called 'gibor' rune (a form of **g** which List connected with the esoteric meanings of the swastika); and a bindrune consisting of **t** and one of the Scandinavian forms of **o**, ᛜ. The **s**-runes, like the 'double lightning bolt' emblem, represent the name of the SS itself, as well as the spurious rune-name *sig* 'victory', invented by List. List claimed that the power of this rune was expressed in an ancient Aryan greeting, *sal und sig* 'hail and victory'. The Germanenorden, a political occult organization founded in 1912 by List's followers, adopted the greeting in the form *Sieg Heil!* and carried it over into the NSDAP, with which many Germanenorden members were involved.

Not everyone in the Nazi hierarchy shared Wiligut's and Himmler's fondness for the esoteric. Hitler, though evidently happy to exploit runic symbols for political purposes, was not personally interested in the occult. The quasi-Masonic trappings and rituals of the SS were just one feature of the complex Nazi State. Nonetheless, runic symbols and swastikas were potent symbols of this State and its organizations, which pervaded every area of society, and the meanings attached to these symbols are based on those proposed by List and/or Wiligut.

After the Second World War, runes fell out of fashion for some time due to their association with Nazi oppression and terror; but a renewed interest in rune-magic was already beginning in the 1950s, and since the 1980s the use of runes for divination has become ever more popular. There is not enough space in this book to look in detail at the enormous amount of modern popular literature on rune-magic; but almost all of it relies on the same key idea promoted by List: that runes are sacred symbols whose forms, names and sounds act as a focus for supernatural energies. In many cases, specific meanings in modern rune-magic books and websites are taken from List – such as the belief that **þ** (*þorn, þurs*) is associated with the god Thor, or that **s** means 'victory'.

That runes are one of the common trappings of fantasy literature – especially, but by no means exclusively, literature set in worlds inspired by Norse mythology – is largely due to the enduring popularity of Tolkien's writings. However, their appearances and function in fantasy stories owe far more to the modern pagan (and ultimately Listian) portrayal of runes as magic symbols with powers linked to their shapes, names and sounds.

As a runologist, I can do little more than repeat what others have said about the functions of runic characters. It is common in literate cultures for writing to be used in magical practices, but this does not mean that magical functions are the primary ones, or that the characters themselves are thought by their creators or by their later users to have any inherent magic power. Runes, like the letters of the Greek, Roman and other alphabets, are first and foremost elements of a system of writing. One could take a benign view of the influence of modern paganism on the popular understanding of runes: just as carvers, scribes and antiquarians in Europe's past adapted runic characters for their own purposes, some modern people have done the same. It is hard, though, not to regret the extent to which the modern reinvention of runes as magic symbols has obscured their far more interesting and complex history as written ones.

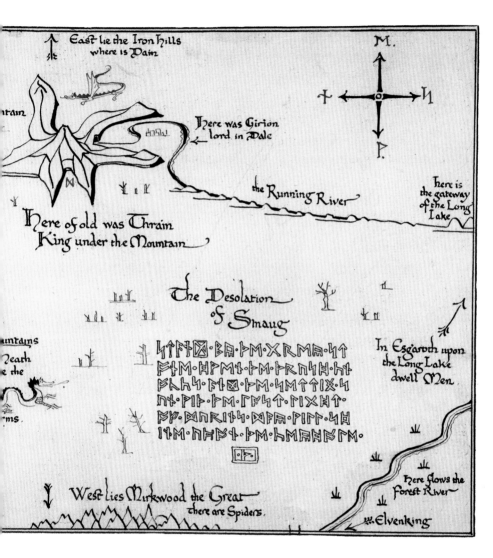

Fig. 37 Map from J.R.R. Tolkien's *The Hobbit* (1937), with modern English text written in Anglo-Saxon runes (chapter 2). Tolkien adapted some of the rune forms, and modified his spelling slightly (for example, feet is written fœt).

Notes

1 *See* Bede's *Ecclesiastical History of the English People*, Book I, chap. 15. In a later passage, Bede counts other groups (including Frisians and Franks) among the invaders, but it is the legendary story of three tribes founding the Anglo-Saxon kingdoms of Bede's own time which endures.

2 'Frisia' here refers to a larger area than the modern Dutch province of Vriesland; it covers coastal regions of what are now the Netherlands, Germany and Denmark. The number of inscriptions known from Frisia is small, and most are difficult to date. We will not be discussing them in detail here: for more information and a handlist of Frisian inscriptions, *see* Looijenga (2003), chapter 9.

3 This is an oversimplification, and not all scholars would agree with this account of the changes in spoken language and the writing system. The linguistic arguments are rather technical, and it would not be appropriate to go into them here.

4 The prehistoric chambered burial site at Maeshowe in Orkney does have runic graffiti, but these were made by Scandinavian crusaders in the mid twelfth century, who broke into the chambers in search of treasure.

Acknowledgements

I should like to thank my parents, Mary and Peter Findell, for their unfailing support and enthusiasm while I was working on this book. Thanks are also due to Emma Poulter, the editor at the British Museum Press, who patiently steered me away from my more esoteric obsessions; this book would have been considerably worse without her insight and feedback. Needless to say, I am fully responsible for any faults or errors to be found here. Lastly, I am grateful to the colleagues whose scholarship makes an introductory book like this possible. In particular, I am deeply indebted to the late Professor R.I. Page, one of the great figures of runology. This book is, in part, a successor to Page's excellent *Runes* (part of the British Museum's series *Reading the Past*). I hope that my own contribution does justice to its eminent predecessor.

Further reading

Books

Some of the following books focus on particular groups
of inscriptions, but most of them deal with more general
topics as well.

Barnes, Michael P., 2012, *Runes: A Handbook*, Woodbridge:
Boydell.

Barnes, Michael, 1994, *The Runic Inscriptions of Maeshowe,
Orkney*, Uppsala: Institutionen för nordiska språk.

Barnes, Michael P. and R.I. Page, 2006, *The Scandinavian
Runic Inscriptions of Britain*, Uppsala: Institutionen for
nordiska språk.

Derolez, R., 1954, *Runica Manuscripta: The English Tradition*,
Bruges: Tempel.

Düwel, Klaus, 2008, 4th edn, *Runenkunde*, Stuttgart:
Metzler.

Flowers, Stephen E., 1986, *Runes and Magic: Magical
Formulaic Elements in the Older Runic Tradition*, New York: Peter
Lang. [Flowers has a background in runology, and is also a

practising occultist who writes under the name Edred Thorsson. This book is based on his doctoral thesis.]

Goodrick-Clarke, Nicholas, 1992, *The Occult Roots of Nazism: Secret Aryan Cults and their Influence on Nazi Ideology*, London: I.B. Tauris.

Goodrick-Clarke, Nicholas, 2002, *Black Sun: Aryan Cults, Esoteric Nazism, and the Politics of Identity*, New York: New York University Press.

Halsall, Maureen, 1981, *The Old English Rune Poem: A Critical Edition*, Toronto: University of Toronto Press. [Also contains texts of the Norwegian and Icelandic rune poems.]

Jansson, Sven B.F., 1987, *Runes in Sweden*, translated by Peter Foote, Stockholm: Gidlunds.

Looijenga, Tineke, 2003, *Texts & Contexts of the Oldest Runic Inscriptions*, Leiden: Brill.

Moltke, Erik, 1985, *Runes and their Origin: Denmark and Elsewhere*, Copenhagen: National Museum of Denmark.

Okasha, Elizabeth, 1971, *Handlist of Anglo-Saxon Non-Runic Inscriptions*, London: Cambridge University Press.

Page, R.I., 1987, *Runes*, London: British Museum Press.

Page, R.I., 1998, 'The Icelandic Rune-Poem', in *Nottingham Medieval Studies*, 42: 1–37.

Page, R.I., 1999, 2nd edn, *An Introduction to English Runes*, Woodbridge: Boydell.

Parsons, David N., 1999, *Recasting the Runes: the Reform of the Anglo-Saxon Futhorc*, Uppsala: Institutionen för nordisk språk. [Parsons makes the case for a deliberate ecclesiastical reform of the futhorc in seventh-century England.]

Seim, Karin Fjellhammer, 1991, 'Middelalderske runesyllaberier', in John Ole Askedal, Harald Bjorvand and Eyvind Fjeld Halvorsen (eds), *Festskrift til Ottar Grønvik*, Oslo: Universitetsforlaget. [Discusses several runic syllabaries from Bergen.]

Spurkland, Terje, 2005, *Norwegian Runes and Runic Inscriptions*, translated by Betsy van der Hoek, Woodbridge: Boydell.

Webster, Leslie, 1999, 'The Iconographic Programme of the Franks Casket' in Jane Hawkes and Susan Mills (eds), *Northumbria's Golden Age*, Stroud: Sutton, pp. 227–46.

Webster, Leslie, 2012, *The Franks Casket*, London: British Museum.

Online resources

The open-access journal *Futhark* publishes current research by runologists worldwide. It is publicly available online: http://www.futhark-journal.com/. There are also links to an extensive bibliography of runological literature.

There are several electronic databases of runic inscriptions:

Runes in Bergen (http://www.nb.no/baser/runer/ribwww/english/runeindex.html). Report and catalogue on the Bergen finds.

Runenprojekt Kiel (http://www.runenprojekt.uni-kiel.de/). A searchable database of Older Futhark inscriptions (available in both German and English, but much of the information on the site is in German only).

Samnordisk runtextdatabas (http://www.runforum.nordis6ka. uu.se/samnord/). A downloadable database of Younger Futhark inscriptions.

Runic material can be found in many other databases of archaeological material. You may find the following particularly helpful:

British Museum's collection search (http://www. britishmuseum.org/research/search_the_collection_ database.aspx).

Early Medieval Corpus of Coin Finds, hosted by the Fitzwilliam Museum, University of Cambridge (http:// www.fitzmuseum.cam.ac.uk/dept/coins/emc/emc_search. php). Portable Antiquities Scheme (http://finds.org.uk/).

Many runic fonts (of varying quality) can be found on the web. This booklet uses the fonts Gullhornet and Gullskoen, designed by Odd Einar Haugen at the University of Bergen. They can be downloaded from the University's website: http://gandalf.aksis.uib.no/Runefonter/.

Timeline

The below shows major developments in the runic writing systems, and inscriptions discussed in the book. All datings are approximate; modern inscriptions and those that are undatable (such as the Selsey fragments, p. 29) have been left out.

Century (AD)	1st	2nd	3rd	4th	5th	6th	7th	8th
	Older Futhark (chap. 1)							
					Gallehus horns (p. 19)	Bad Krozingen brooch (p. 17)	Stentoften stone (p. 78)	
					Kylver stone (p. 16)	'Bateman' brooch (p. 22)		
					Sievern bracteate (p. 78)			
					Anglo-Saxon Futhorc (chap. 2)			
					'Anglo-Frisian' runes (chap. 2, p. 25)			
							'Reformed' Anglo-Saxon Futho[rc]	
					Caistor-by-Norwich bone (p. 34)	Chessell Down pail (p. 86)	'Æpa' coins (p. 33)	Bewcastle cross (p. 41)
					Undley bracteate (p. 26)	Chessell Down scabbard mount (p. 29)	'Benutigo' coins (p. 33)	Franks Casket (p. 44)
						Loveden Hill urn (p. 84)	'Pada' coins (p. 33)	Kingmoor ring (p. 84)
						'Skanomodu' coin (p. 29)		Ruthwell Cross (p. 41)

ap. 2, p. 35)

9th	10th	11th	12th	13th	14th	15th	16th	17th
Younger Futharks (chap. 3)								
Expanded Younger Futharks (with dotted runes and/or additional characters) (chap. 3, p. 59)								
	Jelling stones (p. 62)		Maeshowe graffiti (pp. 65, 100)					
	Lincoln comb-case (p. 60)		Bergen sticks (p. 66)					
	Penrith brooch (p. 57)							
Lancaster cross (p. 41)	Monkwearmouth stone (p. 41)							
	Manchester ring (p. 38)	Sutton brooch (p. 39)						
	Whithorn stone (p. 54)							

Index

Picture credits

Page

2   © miramari/istockphoto

7   © Viktor77/istockphoto

16   SHM 13436_DSC0013 Häll, Stånga sn, Kylver, Go, Inv.nr. 13436; photo: Christer Åhlin/National Historical Museum Stockholm

34   © Norwich Castle Museum and Art Gallery

42   © The Trustees of the British Museum; photo courtesy of Tyne & Wear Archives & Museums

63   © De Agostini Picture Library/A. Dagli Orti/The Bridgeman Art Library

66   Werner Forman Archive/Maritime Museum, Bergen

74   Image courtesy of the University of Leicester

79   Historisches Museum Bremerhaven

96   Kreismuseum Wewelsburg, inventory no. 15907

98   Reprinted by permission of HarperCollins Publishers Ltd. *The Hobbit* © The J R R Tolkien Estate Limited 1937,1965. Copyright in the customised version vests in HarperCollins, UK.